# CONTENTS

# ABOUT THIS BOOK

This *Step by Step Guide* has been produced by the editors of Insight Guides, whose books have set the standard for visual travel guides since 1970. With top-quality photography and authoritative recommendations, this guidebook brings you the very best of Shanghai in a series of 15 tailor-made tours.

## WALKS AND TOURS

The tours in the book provide something to suit all budgets, tastes and trip lengths. As well as covering Shanghai's many classic attractions, the routes track lesser-known sights and up-and-coming areas; there are also excursions for those who want to extend their visit outside the city. The tours embrace a range of interests, so whether you are an art fan, a gourmet, a lover of gardens or have kids to entertain, you will find an option to suit.

We recommend that you read the whole of a tour before setting out. This should help you to familiarise yourself with the route and enable you to plan where to stop for refreshments – options for this are shown in

the 'Food and Drink' boxes, recognisable by the knife-and-fork sign, on most pages.

For our pick of the walks by theme, consult Recommended Tours For ... *(see pp.6–7)*.

### OVERVIEW

The tours are set in context by this introductory section, giving an overview of the city to set the scene, plus background information on food and drink, shopping, entertainment and architecture. A succinct history timeline highlights the key events that have shaped Shanghai over the centuries.

### DIRECTORY

Also supporting the tours is a Directory chapter, comprising a user-friendly, clearly organised A–Z of practical information, our pick of where to stay while you are in the city and select restaurant listings; these eateries complement the more low-key cafés and restaurants that feature within the tours and are intended to offer a wider choice for evening dining. Also included here are some nightlife listings.

**Above**: the Huangpu River at night; the national flag flies over the Bund; shoppers walk past Metro City mall in Xujiahui; a traditional door handle at the Longhua Temple; inside the Jade Buddha Temple.

## The Authors

Principal author **Tina Kanagaratnam** has lived in Shanghai since 1997, where she works as the CEO for communications consulting firm AsiaMedia. Her writing has appeared in numerous publications in China and abroad, including *Shanghai Daily*, *The Financial Times* and *The Washington Post*. Co-founder of editorial consultancy Scribes of the Orient (www.scribesoftheorient.com), **Amy Fabris-Shi** helped to compile the listings and the Overview section.

Thanks to the **Information Office of Shanghai Municipality** for their support with the project.

## Margin Tips
Shopping tips, historical facts, handy hints and information on activities help visitors to make the most of their time in Shanghai.

## Feature Boxes
Notable topics are highlighted in these special boxes.

## Key Facts Box
This box gives details of the distance covered on the tour, plus an estimate of how long it should take. It also states where the route starts and finishes, and gives key travel information such as which days are best to do the route or handy transport tips.

## Route Map
Detailed cartography shows the tour clearly plotted with numbered dots. For more detailed mapping, see the pull-out map slotted inside the back cover.

## Footers
Look here for the tour name, a map reference and the main attraction on the double-page.

## Food and Drink
Recommendations of where to stop for refreshment are given in these boxes. The numbers prior to each restaurant/café name link to references in the main text. Restaurants in the Food and Drink boxes are plotted on the maps.

The $ signs at the end of each entry reflect the approximate cost of a two-course meal for one, with an alcoholic drink. These should be seen as a guide only. Price ranges, also quoted on the inside back flap for easy reference, are:

| | |
|---|---|
| $$$ | over RMB 200 |
| $$ | RMB 100–200 |
| $ | RMB 50–100 |

## FOOD AND DRINK

There is a vast range to choose from in what is one of the world's great culinary centres. Try authentic local food in the Old City or Xintiandi (tours 5, 6), or refined European at M on the Bund (tour 1).

# RECOMMENDED TOURS FOR...

### ARCHITECTURE

Shanghai is a city with a fabulous range of architecture, from wonderful early 20th-century Art Deco (tours 1, 2 and 7) to lane houses (tour 6) and dramatic modern skyscrapers (tours 1, 11 and 12).

### TEMPLES

The colourful Jade Buddha Temple (tour 9) and classical Longhua Pagoda (tour 10) are highlights, while Xiahai Temple (tour 8) feels utterly authentic.

### SHOPPING

Nanjing Road West (tour 4) is famous for its luxury shops, while to the south are Xintiandi and Huaihai Road (tours 6 and 7). The Ming-style bazaar in the Old City (tour 5) and M50 Art District (tour 9) are great for souvenirs.

### CHILDREN

Across the river from the city centre, the Pudong district (tour 11) has a cluster of child-friendly attractions. Kids will also enjoy trips out of town to the gardens of Suzhou (tour 14) and the beautiful "water town" of Tongli (tour 13).

## HISTORY BUFFS

To get an authentic feel for the city's past, visit the former residences of Sun Yat-sen, Zhou En-lai and Soong Ching Ling in the former French Concession (tour 7), or explore the old streets behind the Bund (tour 2).

## ART ENTHUSIASTS

The main draw is the inspirational M50 Art District (tour 9). For a more systematic viewing, art fans will want to see the Shanghai Art Museum and the Museum of Contemporary Art (tour 3), which showcases the country's increasingly high-profile modern art.

## MUSEUMS

The Shanghai Museum on People's Square (tour 3) is a great place to learn about China's long history, while the Jewish Refugees Museum (tour 8) is well worth going out of your way to see.

## PARKS AND GARDENS

People's Park (tour 3) and Fuxing Park (tour 7) provide welcome green space, while further afield Suzhou and Hangzhou (tours 14 and 15) are famed for their classical gardens.

## VIEWS OF PAST AND PRESENT

Make your way over to Pudong (tour 11) and its gargantuan glass-and-steel towers, with views back across the Huangpu River to the 1930s Bund (tour 1).

# OVERVIEW

An overview of Shanghai's geography, customs and culture, plus illuminating background information on food and drink, shopping, entertainment, architecture and history.

# INTRODUCTION

*Bold, brash Shanghai is China's glamour city, where the faded glory of its treaty port history exists hand-in-glove with a soaring skyline and a brilliant future. Prepare to be dazzled.*

Spoil of the Opium Wars, Shanghai was opened to trade in 1842 and subsequently carved up into concessions by foreigners from around the world – an experiment that gave the city its global soul, its thirst for progress and its knack for international commerce. However, such foreign dominance also created a cauldron for resentment, and the Chinese Communist Party held its first meeting here in 1921. Revolution marched alongside old Shanghai's decadent ways, finally winning over the city in May 1949. Since the beginning of the era of "reform and opening up" in 1978, Shanghai has been on a vast growth trajectory, transforming its skyline and economy, building, booming and innovating. The result? A new global city for a new century.

The tours in this book, arranged geographically, take in the different parts of the multilayered Shanghai story – old and new, international and Chinese, business and cultural.

## NAVIGATING THE CITY

Shanghai borders the East China Sea to the east, Hangzhou Bay to the south, and the provinces of Jiangsu and Zhejiang to the west, and the limits of this maritime city's neighbourhoods are also defined by its waterways. The Huangpu River separates Shanghai's newest district, Pudong ("east of the Huangpu") from the rest of the city, Puxi ("west of the Huangpu", pronounced "poo-shee"). The Suzhou Creek divides Puxi's thriving heart from its quieter northern suburbs.

Shanghai Municipality covers roughly 6,340 sq km (2,450 sq miles), within which lie its 17 districts. New district boundaries have been drawn, but the shape and feel of the old foreign settlements and Nanshi ("the old Chinese City") are still discernible. Streets run north to south and east to west in grid-like fashion, except for oval-shaped Nanshi, which follows the lines of the old city wall, and People's Square, defined by the ghost of the old racetrack. The major streets run the length of the city and have directional tags: Huaihai Road West, Central and East, for example. Buildings are usually numbered sequentially (but not always); odd numbers on one side of the street and even numbers on the other; the numbering on residential lanes *(longtang)* that run off the

**Five-Star Fare**
Shanghai taxi drivers all have a star rating, which should be displayed on their dashboard-mounted photo-ID card: three stars or above means that the driver has taken city-administered tests, while five stars means they're supposed to be able to speak some English. You may call English hotline on 962288 for assistance if necessary. Check the rating before you get in – you don't want a no-star!

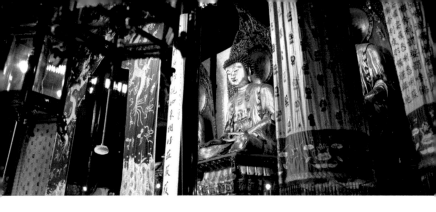

main streets bears no relation to the main street numbering.

The 98km (61-mile) outer ring road, the A20, takes a lap outside the city limits, while the inner ring Zhongshan Road loops around the perimeter of Puxi and Pudong, changing its name in Pudong and east Hongkou before turning back into Zhongshan Road. The city is bisected from east to west by the Yan'an Road Elevated Highway. Crossing the Huangpu River to Pudong from Puxi can be done via ferry, metro, 12 bridges including Nanpu, Yangpu and Lupu, or 13 tunnels.

Street signs are written in pinyin romanisation (or in some cases, in English) and Chinese characters, but most locals and taxi drivers know streets only by their Chinese names. Public transportation is modern, clean, efficient and wide-reaching. It's also fairly accessible for foreigners in that most signage and announcements are in both Chinese and English (bus stop signs are the one exception). However, very little English is spoken by drivers and other transport workers.

### HISTORY AND ARCHITECTURE

Shanghai's history stretches back to the year 751, when Huating County was officially recognised. By 1292, the central government had established Shanghai County, acknowledged as a direct ancestor of contemporary Shanghai. The character of Shanghai as we know it today, however, was most profoundly shaped in the aftermath of the first Opium War in 1842. The treaty that ended that war divided the city into international concessions and brought in a cosmopolitan mix of traders, adventurers and people from around the world fleeing from poverty, revolution and war. Fortunes were made (and lost), and Shanghai began to develop the glamorous sheen and business acumen that it retains today. *For key dates see p.24.*

*Soaring Skyline*

This influx also exerted a profound influence on the city's built environment. Architects from China and around the world created buildings in international styles. Neoclassical, Tudor Revival, Mediterranean, Italianate and most notably Art Deco all feature in Shanghai's landscape. Even the city's domestic *longtang* lanes and *shikumen* houses are an East–West hybrid, unique to Shanghai. *See p.22.*

Shanghai's economic rise since the mid-1990s echoes the 1930s boom with a brand-new skyline and a particular fondness for skyscrapers. The city has thousands of high-rises, with thousands more planned, and three of the world's ten tallest buildings rise up proudly (the Shanghai Tower, World Financial Centre and Jinmao Tower).

**Above from far left:** looking down on the city of Shanghai; lanterns hang inside the Jade Buddha Temple.

## CLIMATE

Shanghai's northern subtropical monsoon climate means plenty of rainfall during the summer months, and four distinct seasons: a hot, humid summer; a damp, cold winter; and crisp, if brief, spring and autumn, which are the best times to visit. *See p.95.*

## THE SHANGHAINESE

Shanghai's population of 23 million is made up of 14.12 million registered Shanghai residents and a further 9 million with household registrations outside the city. The city's burgeoning expatriate population – more than 164,000 from around the world – lends the city a vibrantly cosmopolitan feel.

Shanghainese are considered to be smart, hip – and a little arrogant. The men have a reputation for being shrewd businessmen, but docile at home – Shanghai men famously, uncomplainingly, carry their girlfriends' handbags. The women are just as sharp as the men when it comes to business, and very well turned out. Impressions count a great deal here: visitors from Beijing chuckle that even the undersides of the city's elevated highways are painted. Shanghainese are conspicuous consumers, with a passion for upmarket brands, luxury cars and fine dining. The city's history of amalgamating East and West gave rise to a style called *hai pai*, which

translates today to an openness to Western ideas and customs.

## LOCAL CUSTOMS

Shanghai has a relentless big-city pace, rising early and going to bed late. By 7am, the t'ai chi practitioners and ballroom dancers are going through their paces in the parks, and the markets are buzzing. Offices, banks and museums are open by 9am, while shops open between 10 and 11am, and restaurants begin opening for lunch by 11.30am.

Shanghai has a lively nightlife scene, and the city's bars and clubs stay open into the early hours, with some remaining open all night.

*Speaking English*

The city has the largest population of English-speakers in the country, yet there are still numerous situations in which very little English is spoken – these include taxis, markets, shopping centres, public transport (though the signs are bilingual), police, local hospitals (though some have a "foreigners' section") and some government offices. In most public places, however, you will probably find English-speaking locals who are usually happy to help.

Besides an English newspaper *(Shanghai Daily)* and a TV channel with 24-hour English and Japanese programmes, there is also a service hotline (tel: 962288) with 15 languages to assist foreigners in Shanghai.

**Preserving the Past**
Many of Shanghai's historic buildings have "Heritage Architecture" signs, but this doesn't necessarily mean that the building is protected. However, the city does have historic preservation advocates, who have created a protected buildings list and 12 preservation zones – one of the reasons that this rapidly developing city retains its cache of historic buildings.

## POLITICS & ECONOMICS

Shanghai is known for sending its politicians on to bigger jobs in Beijing. Jiang Zemin and Zhu Rongji are both former mayors who went on to become president and premier respectively. Xi Jinping, a former Shanghai Communist Party Secretary – the top-ranked position – is now the General Secretary of the CPC Central Committee.

### China's Financial Capital

Shanghai is the nation's thriving economic heart and its financial capital. With just 0.06% of the nation's land area, it contributes 4.1% of China's GDP, and the value of its imports and exports accounted for 12.4% of the nation's total in 2011.

Per capita GDP in 2011 was US$12,784, on a par with a medium developed country. In recent years, the city has seen unprecedented growth year-on-year, and even as the pace slows as the economy matures – to 8.2% in 2011, lower than the national average of 9.2% – the overall optimism continues. But the government has not been complacent. Transitioning the economy from an investment-driven to a consumption-driven basis, and from a manufacturing base to a more innovation-oriented society, have both been key priorities.

The government's massive investments during the 2008 financial crisis and Expo kept the Shanghai economy vibrant, but recognizing that a more sustainable model was needed to the long-term, it is now focused on the transition to a consumption-driven economy even at the cost of lower GDP growth rate. The second area of long-term focus is the movement from being the world's factory – ie manufacturing – to a more creative, or innovation-oriented society: from "Made in China " to "Invented in China ". These transitions will help the government achieve its goal of becoming an international economic, financial, trade and shipping center by 2020.

Hand-in-hand with the economic policies designed to assure a well-off society, the government is also working to accelerate social development with the focus of improving livelihoods. To date, they have provided 17-million square meters of low-income housing, and the average living space of urben residents has been improved to 17 square meters. More resources have been invested in community nursing services for the elderly, and significant reform of the city's medi-care system is on the way.

What this means for the visitor is that Shanghai offers luxuries that few other Chinese cities can afford, with rates to match. Top-end hotels and restaurants command international price tags – and these are now being targeted more and more at the increasingly wealthy domestic market.

**Above from far left:** shoppers on Nanjing West Road; the Shanghai Science and Technology Museum; playing Chinese chess (xiangqi), People's Park.

# FOOD AND DRINK

*Whether you're after an early-morning breakfast of crispy fried crullers or a late-night snack of plump steamed dumplings, you've come to the right place – Shanghai is a city that loves to eat 24 hours a day.*

For sheer variety alone, Shanghai is one of the best places to chow down in the whole of China. Dining choices range from miniature hole-in-the-wall eateries, where you squat on tiny stools to slurp your meal from plastic bowls, to swanky restaurants helmed by global culinary stars.

Over the past decade, famous chefs have poured in from around the world, transforming Shanghai into an international dining destination. The diversity is breathtaking, with culinary treats on offer from Africa, Brazil, India, Europe and Southeast Asia. There's also an impressive array of Chinese regional cuisines – from Yunnan to Xinjiang and Guangdong to Dongbei – plus, of course, plenty of Shanghai's own oily-sweet fare.

## SHANGHAINESE CUISINE

Throughout most of China's history Shanghai was a muddy fishing village, while nearby cities such as Hangzhou and Nanjing, both former capitals of China, were famous for their beauty, culture, sophistication and fine food. Without any great palaces or emperors to inspire its cuisine, the Shanghainese instead turned to the bays and estuaries of the Yangtze Delta for their daily meals. Authentic local cuisine still relies heavily on freshwater crabs, eels, river fish, shrimps and other shallow-water creatures, along with traditional Chinese staples of chicken and pork, and a rich selection of seasonal local vegetables.

With its country roots, the preparation of Shanghainese cuisine is far less complex than that of its Cantonese or Beijing cousins, relying on soy sauce, oil and sugar for flavour, and featuring just three major methods of preparation: *hong shao* or red-cooked

**Tipping Point**
Tipping isn't standard practice in Shanghai, but it's becoming more common. Hotels and some high-end restaurants now add a 10–15% service charge to the bill.

## Magic Markets

Eating in Shanghai is still refreshingly defined by the seasons, and the city's fresh produce markets and corner fruit stores are the go-to places for raw ingredients. These lively neighbourhood markets are far removed from the bland supermarket experience – be prepared to encounter just-plucked vegetables with muddy roots, huge sides of pork, and live fish and chickens. Seasonal favourites to look out for include fat bamboo shoots in spring, *yangmei* berries and juicy white peaches in summer, and sweet miniature mandarins in winter.

(with sugar and soy sauce), stewed or simply stir-fried with ginger and spring onions. One of the city's most iconic dishes is *hong shao* pork, fatty cubes of pork belly stewed in a soy sauce marinade until they practically melt in the mouth.

Shanghai's famous flair is better revealed in its cold dishes. Expect artistically arranged hors d'œuvres of dazzling variety, from plates of julienned vinegary pickles or tiny live shrimps served in rice wine, to spiced broad beans, "drunken" chicken marinated in wine, and sweet wheat gluten *(kao fu)*.

As diners become more and more health-conscious, modern Shanghainese cuisine is starting to veer away from its overly dark and oily origins, and dishes at upscale Shanghai restaurants are less fatty and sweet than they once were. Meanwhile, the city is also starting to embrace the more sophisticated cuisine of Hangzhou, which is lighter and brighter, with more of a reliance on freshness and quick cooking.

Vegetarians can find dining in regular Chinese restaurants a challenge, as even vegetable dishes tend to be cooked in meat stock or contain small bits of meat. However, a number of Buddhist restaurants, such as Gongdelin, offer large menus of meat-free Chinese dishes, often using tofu and mushrooms in ingenious ways to mimic typical meat dishes.

Left: waiters juggle orders of dumplings at Nanxiang Steamed Bun Restaurant inside Yu Yuan Garden.

### Street Food and Dumplings

Shanghai dumplings are the city's favourite street food snack, and streetside stands are easily identified by their cylindrical bamboo steamers emitting fragrant puffs of steam.

Shanghai boasts two signature dumpling specialities: *shengjian*

*mantou* are pan-fried in giant, crusty black pans. Filled with pork and scalding broth with crispy bottoms, they are also known by their English nickname, "potstickers". *Xiaolong bao* are smaller, more delicate steamed dumplings that look like translucent money pouches and are filled with pork, broth and, sometimes, luxurious crab roe. The best places to sample *xiaolong bao* are at Din Tai Fung and Nan Xiang, while Yang's Fry Dumplings sizzles up the finest potstickers.

Breakfast is almost always eaten on the run, with *youtiao*, a long fried doughnut (or cruller), washed down with freshly brewed soybean milk, a local favourite. For the Shanghainese version of a breakfast burrito, try a *jianbing* pancake filled with fried egg, a crispy bean curd sheet, coriander and chilli sauce, cooked on a steaming griddle and rolled up for takeaway. Steamed *baozi* bread rolls are also eaten from big bamboo steamers, with a choice of fillings including pork, vegetables or sweet red bean paste.

Snacks and street food are available on virtually every corner in Shanghai, but the best selection can be found at Yu Garden Bazaar, where hordes of Chinese tourists patiently wait in line to sample the treats on offer. As well as those mentioned above, you can't miss the stench of another local favourite – *chou doufu*, or smelly bean curd. These little deep-fried cubes of fermented bean curd from Fenxian County on

## Local Brews

Shanghai's teahouses serve some of the finest teas in the world. Two of the most popular brews are *longjing* (Dragon Well) green tea from the hills of nearby Hangzhou, and rich black *pu'er* tea from Yunnan province. The *longjing* tea is mild, sweet and refreshing, while *pu'er* is rich, black and fully fermented, with an intensely smoky taste and a pronounced caffeine kick.

Chinese beer is cheap and popular, with Tsingtao a reliable light pilsner. Sometimes people in Shanghai will drink *huang jiu*, or yellow wine, a sweet, golden-amber liquid made from glutinous rice. The best *huang jiu* comes from nearby Shaoxing. A more lethal beverage is *bai jiu*, or Chinese white liquor. Consumed from small glasses generally as a shot after a toast of "*gan bei*" (cheers), this transparent distilled grain spirit has a 40–60% alcohol content and is an acquired taste.

Grape wine is rapidly gaining popularity too. China is one of the world's biggest importers of wine, but now a handful of local Chinese wineries, such as Grace Vineyards, are producing some excellent home-grown vintages. A good sommelier will be able to recommend the best Chinese wines – the cheaper bottles are not recommended. Many upscale restaurants, bars and hotels have truly impressive cellars stocked with a global selection of wines. In Shanghai, the most expensive grands crus regularly get popped in a show of extravagance.

the outskirts of Shanghai are a somewhat acquired taste, but locals love their pungent flavour, especially when dipped in chilli sauce.

## Hairy Crabs

Arguably Shanghai's best-loved seasonal gourmet delicacy is the hairy crab. Every year from mid-October to the end of December, when the crabs are ripe with milt or roe, huge crowds of people drive to the shores of nearby Yangcheng Lake to catch and eat these critters, so named because of their down-covered claws. The crabs are also available in restaurants and markets across Shanghai, where they are steamed and served with a sauce of ginger, vinegar and sugar. Although no bigger than a human fist and very fiddly to eat, their meat and roe are sweet and buttery, with a rich flavour and superb velvety texture. Hairy crabs are considered to be "cooling" to the body, so sherry-like Shaoxing wine is served to rebalance the body's yin and yang.

### UNRIVALLED DINING SCENE

Shanghai's international culinary scene is so spectacular that it is the only city in China to have its own Zagat Guide. New restaurants open every month, and one local publication lists over 40 different types of cuisine in its restaurant directory.

Shanghai is a city of immigrants, and its restaurants represent a veritable microcosm of China. Along with the major cuisines – Cantonese, Beijing, Sichuan – are endless variations in between. Sichuan hotpot *(huoguo)* restaurants, at which a pot of chilli-laced bubbling soup, sitting over a flame, is used for dipping and cooking vegetables and meats, are popular during the cold winters, as is Cantonese dim sum for an elegant brunch or high tea.

Due to long working days and small home kitchens, local residents generally prefer to eat out for most meals. Good restaurants tend to be packed at mealtimes, so book ahead or be prepared to wait. Prices vary wildly, as does food quality. Food cleanliness and "fake" ingredients are a genuine concern at some places, so be sure to stick to the more popular or recommended restaurants and food stalls, and be aware that you are probably getting what you pay for at very cheap dives.

## Café Culture

Café culture has a long heritage in Shanghai, and between classical Chinese teahouses and the European-influenced coffee shops and bakeries, there is a wealth of unique cafés for a reviving cuppa and people-watching. When you've had your fill of noodles, café chains such as Wagas and Element Fresh have multiple stores around the city offering fresh salads and good coffee, plus free WiFi access.

**Above from far left:** crabs are a perennial local favourite; a half-empty wooden bowl of dumplings at Nanxiang Steamed Bun Restaurant restaurant, Yu Yuan Garden.

**Dinner Time**
Traditionally, Chinese mealtimes are on the early side, with dinner eaten around 6pm or 6.30pm. As a result, kitchens at Chinese restaurants tend to close early too, with mobile kebab grills and noodle stands materialising to cater to the late-night crowds. There are exceptions, though – Cantonese diner Cha's, Taiwanese Chamant and French supperclub Mr & Mrs Bund carry on serving into the early hours.

# SHOPPING

*Shanghai is a bona fide shoppers' paradise. You can find almost anything in the city's plentiful markets, malls and boutiques, from traditional items such as fine tea, porcelain and Art Deco antiques to the latest designer fashions and contemporary art.*

Shopping in Shanghai was once limited to cheap knock-offs and kitschy souvenirs, but now big-name global luxury brands are courting the city's new wealthy classes with opulent flagship stores and China-inspired product lines. In 2012, Louis Vuitton opened its first China Maison and largest Shanghai store across four levels at Plaza 66, while New York "Jeweller to the Stars" Harry Winston unveiled its largest global salon in a freestanding pavilion at Xintiandi.

Local designers and niche labels are also getting in on the act, taking advantage of the dominant consumer spirit and easy access to raw materials to launch an array of exciting new brands and boutiques. These can be found dotted around the former French Concession and the streets behind the Bund.

Add to this traditional arts and crafts shops, antiques markets with one-off finds, and the city's famous custom tailors and silk purveyors ready to whip up a bespoke wardrobe, and you might want to consider bringing along an extra suitcase for your Shanghai purchases – or buying one, of course.

## SHOPPING BY AREA

Shanghai's main shopping streets are Nanjing Road and Huaihai Road. The eastern pedestrianised end of Nanjing Road is usually mobbed by local and out-of-town Chinese shoppers at weekends, while Nanjing Road (W) and Huaihai Road are studded with marble malls, luxury boutiques and fast fashion outlets.

### Shanghai Chic

The traditional lanes and *shikumen* houses of Xintiandi are now a hotbed of big designer brands. For funkier fashions, head over to the adjoining Xintiandi Style mall (245 Madang Road), where hip young designers from Shanghai and across Asia showcase their latest collections.

In the former French Concession, the narrow residential lanes of Tianzifang (Lane 210 Taikang Road) are packed with local designer boutiques, trinket stalls and alfresco cafés – it's a great place to pick up some one-off souvenirs and while away an afternoon. Look out for hand-embroidered ethnic-styled accessories at Harvest

**Shop 'til You Drop**
Opposite the smart IFC mall in Pudong is one of China's largest malls, the Superbrand Mall (168 Lujiazui Road W), featuring a staggering 13 storeys of high-street labels, plus an Egyptian-themed cineplex and an ice-skating rink.

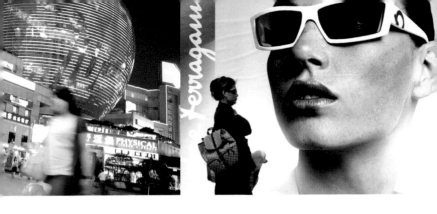

Studio (Suite 18, Bldg 3, Lane 210 Taikang Road), cosy gear spun from sustainably sourced yak down at Shokay (Bldg 9, 274 Taikang Road), and photographic prints of Shanghai scenes at Deke Erh Art Centre (No. 2, Lane 210 Taikang Road).

The streets around the Bund also harbour some gems among the showier boutiques. Check out Suzhou Cobblers (Room 101, 17 Fuzhou Road) for a pair of handcrafted silk slippers, Blue China White (Room 103, 17 Fuzhou Road) offering hand-painted Jingdezhen porcelain tableware, and Annabel Lee Shanghai (No. 1, Lane 8 Zhongshan East Road) for its gorgeous selection of lush silk accessories.

Across the river in Pudong, the sparkling IFC mall (8 Century Avenue) is one of the city's best, and is home to an excellent food court and supermarket in the basement.

## Art and Antiques

The M50 art district at 50 Moganshan Road beside Suzhou Creek is the place to pick up a choice piece of contemporary Chinese art from the myriad galleries and artists' workshops. Vanguard Gallery (Bldg 4; www.vanguardgallery.com), OV Gallery (Room 207; tel: 5465 7768; www.ovgallery.com) and ShanghART (Building 16; tel: 6359 3923; www.shanghartgallery.com) come recommended.

Dongtai Road Antique Market, close to the Old City, is a delightful street market lined with outdoor hawkers selling fun repro-antique trinkets and "Mao-morabilia" that make great souvenirs. Be prepared to haggle. For genuine Art Deco antiques, duck into the established stores set back from the street.

Shanghai is close to China's freshwater pearling areas, and you can pick up well-priced pearls, and have them strung, at Hongqiao Pearl City (3721 Hongmei Road). Porcelain and other wares can be purchased at the Shanghai Jingdezhen Porcelain Store (212 Shanxi Road N), while tea and Yixing pots are plentiful at the Shanghai Huangshan Tea Company (605 Huaihai Road C).

## Custom Clothing

Custom tailor shops abound in Shanghai. One of the best – with top-drawer prices to match – is the French Tailor (7 Dongping Road; tel: 5465 2468). Equally fine threads can be had from Dave's Custom Tailoring (No.6, Lane 288 Wuyuan Road; tel: 5404 0001).

At the cheap and cheerful end of the spectrum is the South Bund Fabric Market (399 Lujiabang Road), a three-storey warren of small stores selling bolts of material in every guise. Tailors stand ready with scissors and thread once you've made your choice and can whip up custom-fit copies of your own clothing or of one of their designs in as little as 24 hours.

**Above from far left:** a Cultural Revolution-era poster at Dongtai Road Antique Marktet; shoppers walk past Metro City shopping mall in Xujiahui; a woman walks outside Ferragamo Boutique on Nanjing Road West.

**Above:** items for sale at the Dongtai Road Antique Market: a Chairman Mao watch and a small lion statue.

# ENTERTAINMENT

*With a string of glamorous bars and a world-renowned party scene, it's easy to understand why Shanghai has been dubbed "the city that never sleeps". There's also a calendar bursting with performances, festivals and cultural activities, and a fine array of art galleries.*

China's most cosmopolitan city prides itself on its spectacular arts and entertainment scene. Huge investment in cultural venues in recent years means Shanghai now has several world-class theatres and concert halls, including the Mercedes-Benz Arena, the Shanghai Culture Plaza and the Oriental Arts Centre. These, along with charming heritage venues such as the Shanghai Concert Hall, Yifu Theatre and Majestic Theatre, regularly stage musicals, concerts, dance performances, Chinese opera, drama and even rock concerts throughout the year. There's plenty of foreign star talent on offer too, from Yo-Yo Ma to Usher and *The Lion King*.

## DANCE & ACROBATICS

Local talent includes the excellent Shanghai Ballet and the Jin Xing Modern Dance Company. A must-see is the Shanghai Acrobatic Troupe, justly renowned for its breathtaking contortions and stunts mixed with multimedia technology – the group performs at Circus World and the Shanghai Gong Stage near the Bund.

## MUSIC & OPERA

Founded in 1952, the Shanghai Philharmonic Orchestra has since carved out a reputation for solid musicianship. For a more local flavour, check out the Shanghai Chinese Orchestra – it was China's first large-scale modern ensemble made up of traditional Chinese instruments. The orchestra performs regular Shanghai concerts and tours internationally. The centre for Chinese opera is the Yifu Theatre. Occasionally, the oldest form of Chinese opera (Kunju), which originated in the nearby town of Kunshan, is performed here too.

## FILM

Despite the abundance of cheap counterfeit DVDs, cineplexes continue to be popular. Most Chinese films are shown without subtitles. Hollywood blockbusters are screened in English with Chinese subtitles at selected cinemas; otherwise they're dubbed into Chinese. China's booming film industry is currently the world's second-largest, with a huge movie-making output and

**Look and Book**
For a detailed list of performances in Shanghai, check out www.culture.sh.cn. You can book tickets via the website hotline (6217 2426) or direct with the venue.

new cinemas being opened across the country. Hollywood is also regularly inspired by Shanghai – scenes from the 2012 James Bond movie *Skyfall* were shot in the city.

## ART GALLERIES

The largest concentration of galleries is at M50 (No.50 Moganshan Road). Clustered here in old warehouses by Suzhou Creek are some of the city's most interesting art galleries showcasing cutting-edge works. Entrance to the galleries is usually free, and most are closed on Sundays or Mondays (it's best to call ahead to confirm).

The city's major art festival, the Shanghai Biennale, takes place in even-numbered years, while the privately run ShContemporary, held in September, features cutting-edge Chinese contemporary art.

## NIGHTLIFE

Shanghai really comes alive after dark. The more upscale bars are along the Bund, Xintiandi and dotted throughout the former French Concession. Other popular bar strips can be found along Yongfu Road and Hengshan Road.

While Shanghai's live music scene is not as vibrant as Beijing's, the city does manage to hold its own. A handful of underground clubs, including the Shelter and Yuyintang, host live rock gigs and celebrity DJs, but jazz has been king in Shanghai since the 1920s. The city has several first-rate jazz clubs that attract top musicians from China and around the world – JZ Club and House of Blues & Jazz are favourites. Drinks prices are comparable to other major world cities.

Shanghai's free listings magazines and nightlife websites provide extensive bar and nightclub listings as well as current events. The most reliable sources of information are www.SmartShanghai.com and City Weekend (www.cityweekend.com.cn). For more on nightlife, *see p.118.*

## FESTIVALS

The city hosts a wide range of annual festivals, generally held during the milder months of spring and autumn. Traditional festivals such as Chinese New Year (January/February) and the Mid-Autumn Festival (September) involve fireworks, temple visits and other traditional celebrations.

Government-sponsored cultural festivals, including the Shanghai International Film Festival (June), Shanghai Fashion Week (April/October) and Shanghai Biennale (October), are steadily growing in stature. Well-run independent festivals to look out for are the Shanghai Literary Festival and JUE Music + Art (both held in March), and the biannual Eco Design Fair (April/November).

**Above from far left:** ballet at the Shanghai International Culture and Art Festival.; Shanghai Peking Opera Troupe

# ARCHITECTURE

*Mixing Art Deco, Postmodernist, Song Dynasty, Tudor, uber-modern and just plain kitsch, Shanghai is a stimulating showcase of architectural treasures that will take your breath away.*

Even world-weary sophisticates find themselves catching their breath the first time they glimpse Shanghai's skyline. The city has undergone the biggest urban building boom the world has known, and the sheer scale and speed of reconstruction are astounding. This urban boom echoes another one a century earlier, and the juxtaposition of avant-garde glass-and-steel towers and historic brick buildings provides a wonderfully arresting sight.

## CONCESSION ERA

For 40 years after the Communists' victory in 1949, construction virtually halted in Shanghai. Thus, when restrictions on development were lifted in the early 1990s, the city was a time capsule of pre-1949 architecture. While it's sad to see so many historic buildings razed to make way for highways and sky-scrapers, it's important to remember that the city has always been about being modern. In the 1920s and 30s, modernity meant Art Deco. Known for its ability to weave outside ideas into local culture, Shanghai adapted the born-in-the-West style to China, and it became a symbol of the city.

**Beyond the Bund**
Some say the space-age Pearl Oriental Tower, just opposite the Bund, was built to divert attention from the latter – a symbol of the city's "humiliating" colonial past. If so, the tower has proved to be a resounding success.

*Lane Houses*

The most typical Shanghainese archi-tectural form is the *lilong* or *longtang* (lane) neighbourhood. First built during the Taiping Rebellion (1853–64), when affluent Chinese from nearby provinces fled to Shanghai and the safety of the Concessions, *longtangs* are a uniquely Shanghainese hybrid: based on the southern Chinese courtyard house, the buildings have multiple storeys and Western-style exterior decoration.

Lane neighbourhoods typically cover a city block, with a few entrances from the street that can be locked by iron gates. Within the neighbourhood lanes are arrayed in a matrix pattern, the stone-framed doors *(shikumen)* facing south. These attached dwellings are more than just buildings – they're a way of life. Because the houses are cramped, the lanes are treated as living space, where laundry is done, hair is washed and vegetables are peeled.

*The Concessions*

No visit is complete without a stroll along the Bund, with its striking pano-rama of European buildings: about half of the 24 structures were built in the

1920s, and nine during the previous two decades *(see p.28)*. Most incorporate the neoclassical themes prevalent during the period, including the regal 1923 Pudong Development Bank (built as the Hongkong and Shanghai Bank) and the Waldorf Astoria (built as the Shanghai Club). The most famous is the Art Deco Fairmont Peace Hotel (formerly the Cathay Hotel); the oldest is the former British Consulate (1874).

Old Shanghai did business in the International Settlement, but much preferred to live in the tree-lined French Concession, where the Mediterranean, Tudor and Art Deco homes still stand. Many are private residences, but some are open to the public: the magnificent Shanghai Arts and Crafts Museum *(see p.55)*; Taiyuan Villa, a French Provincial mansion built for the Comte du Pac de Marsoulies; and the former home of the wealthy industrialist Rong family, now the Xuhui Children's Palace *(see p.56)*.

## MODERN SHANGHAI

Shanghai's most successful modern buildings include references to Chinese architecture or push the high-design envelope. The Shanghai Grand Theatre (People's Square Walk) does both – it resembles a hyper-modern transparent temple to the arts, until you realise that its roof pays homage to classical Chinese upturned eaves.

The Shanghai Centre's red columns supporting the entrance portico, meanwhile, are a clear reference to traditional motifs; less obvious is that the shape of the building is the Chinese character for mountain, *shan*.

The pagoda-like Jinmao Tower incorporates both Chinese and Shanghai Art Deco in a modern exterior, while the soaring World Financial Centre has won Shanghai's heart by simply being the tallest.

Postmodern European architects have also been popular: the seagull-inspired Pudong International Airport and the ceramic-and-glass Oriental Arts Centre were both designed by French architect Paul Andreu.

## FUTURE SHANGHAI

The pace of change has been tremendous over the past 15 years, and shows no signs of abating. The largest redevelopment is the 74 sq km (29 sq miles) along the banks of the Huangpu River on the Puxi side, much of which will be green space. The Shiliupu Wharf has been transformed from dingy warehouses to a vibrant waterfront hub of shopping, dining and entertainment. In Hongkou, an international cruise ship terminal has opened, with luxury hotels, shopping and entertainment under way. Finally, a carbon-neutral satellite city is being planned for rural Chongming Island to accommodate the floods of migrants.

**Above:** the Bund waterfront is Shanghai's best-known architectural ensemble.

**Above:** the iconic Pudong skyline

# HISTORY: KEY DATES

*In its transformation from fishing village to bustling trading port and now China's leading city, Shanghai has survived wars, foreign takeovers and 20th-century turmoil.*

| | |
|---|---|
| **4000 BC** | Prehistoric hunter-gatherers settle in the Yangtze Delta. |
| **1000 BC** | A tiny farming and fishing village is established on the banks of the Huangpu River. |
| **AD 500–1300** | Shanghai grows in size and importance, and it develops a trading culture during the Southern Song Dynasty (1127–1279). |
| **1400s** | The Huangpu is dredged several times, setting the stage for commercial success. |
| **1554** | Shanghai builds a wall to protect itself from Japanese pirates; the circular edges of the wall still define the borders of the Old Town. |
| **1685** | The Qing Dynasty opens a customs office, and Shanghai grows in commercial importance, with cotton, silk and tea the key exports. |
| **1839–45** | The British Army invades China and forces it to sign the Treaty of Nanjing, which gives Britain a foreign concession in Shanghai. France and America soon establish concessions of their own. |
| **1851–4** | The Taiping Rebellion rages across China, and Chinese residents pour into Shanghai. |

**Mosquito Press**
In 1900, a Shanghai newspaperman discovered he could sell more papers by including gossip from the city's brothels. News from the brothels gave rise to the institution of the Chinese tabloid or *xiaobao*. Known in English as the "mosquito press", these papers covered the private lives of the city's most famous prostitutes.

**Right:** a Chinese machine-gun crew rests between battles with Japanese forces in 1937.

| | |
|---|---|
| **1850s** | Shanghai's boisterous Golden Age begins, and it becomes one of the fastest-growing and most famous cities on earth. It is rife with crime, but rich in opportunity for both Chinese and Westerners. |
| **1911** | The Qing Dynasty collapses, and a weak and fragmented Nationalist government takes over the Republic of China. |
| **1921** | The Chinese Communist Party is founded in Shanghai; Mao Zedong attends the meeting. |
| **1923** | The Hongkong and Shanghai Bank Building opens on the Bund. |
| **1931–41** | Shanghai becomes a safe haven for some 20,000 Jews fleeing persecution in Europe. |
| **1931–2** | Japan bombs and invades Shanghai, but withdraws under the weight of international pressure. |
| **1937** | Japan bombs and invades Shanghai again, destroying many buildings and driving scores of residents out of the city. |
| **1949** | The Communists win the Chinese Civil War and the People's Republic of China is founded. |
| **1978** | Deng Xiaoping launches the "openings and reforms" era. |
| **1992** | Deng takes his famous "southern tour" to encourage commerce in Shanghai, which he calls the Dragon's Head of the Yangtze Delta. |
| **1994** | Former Shanghai mayor Jiang Zemin becomes president of China. Metro line 1 opens, as does the Oriental Pearl Tower in Pudong, symbol of the new city. |
| **1998** | The Jinmao Tower opens in Pudong. |
| **1999** | Pudong International Airport opens, and the city's elevated highway system is finished. |
| **2001** | Shanghai Cooperation Organisation is founded. Shanghai hosts the 9th APEC Summit. |
| **2002** | Shanghai hosts the first Tennis Masters Cup in China. |
| **2003** | Hu Jintao succeeds Jiang Zemin as president of China. |
| **2004** | Shanghai hosts the first Formula One Grand Prix in China. The high-speed Maglev rail line opens. |
| **2008** | The World Financial Centre building opens in Pudong. |
| **2010** | Shanghai holds the largest World Expo in the fair's history. |
| **2011** | The Shanghai metro becomes the longest in the world, totalling around 420km (260 miles), with more lines under construction. |
| **2012** | The Shanghai Tower overtakes the World Financial Centre as the loftiest skyscraper in the city. When completed in 2014, it will be the second-tallest building in the world, at 632m (2,073ft). |

**Above from far left:**
Shanghai was one of five "treaty" ports opened to British trade in the 19th century; college students dressed as Liberation Army soldiers on National Day.

# WALKS AND TOURS

# THE BUND

*The Bund has been Shanghai's signature sight for over a century. This half-day stroll among its grand, early 20th-century European buildings gives a fascinating insight into the city's Concession-era past.*

---

**DISTANCE** 1.5km (1 mile)
**TIME** A half-day
**START** Huangpu Park
**END** Gutzlaff Signal Tower
**POINTS TO NOTE**

To reach the starting point, take a taxi to Huangpu Park (Huangpu Gongyuan) or the metro to Nanjing East Road (Nanjing Dong Lu), then it's about a 15-minute walk. This tour can be combined with the Behind the Bund tour *(see p.32)* for an in-depth look at the area.

---

Site of the first foreign settlement in Shanghai, the fabled Bund was once home to the most important banks and trading companies in the Far East. Its domes and towers formed the first glimpse of the city for arrivals in the pre-flight age, and the Bund so defined Shanghai that the People's Liberation Army marched its length when they entered the city in 1949. Even its name is a legacy of the British Empire, from the Hindi *band* (river embankment). For some Chinese, the Bund is a reminder of a shameful century of foreign domination (1843–1943),

**Mixed Messages**
The Bund buildings' historic signs offer very little information aside from the name and date of the original building and are of varying accuracy – take them all with a pinch of salt.

but this historic strip has now entered a new golden age as a prime dining, entertainment and shopping hub.

## NORTHERN BUND

Begin at **Huangpu Park ❶** (Huangpu Gongyuan; 500 Zhongshan No. 1 Road; tel: 5308 2636; daily 6am–6pm; free), at the northern end of the Bund. The former Public Garden was built on reclaimed land and opened in 1886, and was famously closed to Chinese (other than nannies of foreign children). A Socialist Realist sculpture stands on the site of the old bandstand, and next to it rises the **Monument to the People's Heroes** (Renmin Yingxiong Jinianbei) – that is, all those who fought to rid China of foreign imperialism.

Cross at the zebra crossing at the foot of Waibaidu Bridge to see the oldest buildings on the Bund, **Nos. 33–53 Waitan Yuan ❷** (daily 9am–6pm). This recently renovated pair of British Colonial beauties was built in the 1870s and served as the British Consulate and the Consul's residence until 1949. The buildings are closed to the public, but visitors can still enjoy the beautiful landscaped gardens.

Continue south past the neighbouring Peninsula Shanghai (Bandao Dajiudian). This new Art Deco Revival hotel marks the return of the Kadoories, one of the great Sephardic Jewish families of old Shanghai, to the city where they made their fortune.

Three doors down is the **House of Roosevelt** (Luosifu) at No. 27, a grand granite-clad building built in 1922 as the Shanghai seat of Jardine Matheson & Co., the most important British trading company in the Far East. Today, it's home to several restaurants and a private club. Be sure to take in the stunning view from the eighth floor of Shanghai old and new.

Another three doors down, the 1937 **Bank of China** ❸ (Zhongguo Yinhang), at No. 23, is the only Bund building with Chinese ornamentation, the only one designed by a Chinese architect (Lu Qianshou) and one of the city's best examples of Chinese Art Deco architecture. It was from its vaults that Nationalist leader Chiang Kai-shek emptied the country's gold reserves and shipped them to Taiwan as he prepared to abandon the mainland in 1949.

*The Peace Hotel*
Right next door at No. 20 stands one of the legends of the Bund, the **Fairmont Peace Hotel** ❹ (Heping Fandian; tel: 6321 6888; www.fairmont.com), opened in 1929 as the luxurious Cathay Hotel by property tycoon Sir Victor Sassoon – scion of

another highly successful Sephardic Jewish family in Shanghai.

Enter on the Nanjing Road side and take the lift to the eighth floor, where some of what made the Cathay a legend remains: the vivid Art Deco ceilings and columns in the Dragon-Phoenix restaurant; the exquisite Lalique sconces lining the hallway to the magnificent ballroom. Charming **Victor's Café**, see ❶①, on the ground floor, has a tempting array of pastries and drinks – and top-notch people-watching seats by the windows.

Returning to the Bund, cross the street and pay your respects to the statue of **Chen Yi**, a Long Marcher and accomplished general who became Shanghai's first post-liberation mayor. He was named China's Foreign Minister in 1959, but was "purged" in 1966 during the Cultural Revolution.

Mount the stairs to the riverside **Bund Promenade** and gaze at the futuristic Pudong skyline. This impressive concentration of skyscrapers includes three of the 10 tallest buildings in the world: the Shanghai Tower (632m/2,073ft, second-tallest), the World Financial

**Above from far left:**
the Bund is attractively lit at night; morning exercises on the Bund Promenade; view from the patio of the Bund Center.

**AKA Waitan**
It's only foreigners who call this historic strip the Bund. For generations, locals have known it as Waitan ("outer shore"); the prosaic name of the street itself is Zhongshan Dong Yi Lu (Zhongshan Road East, section one).

## Food and Drink
**① VICTOR'S CAFÉ**
Fairmont Peace Hotel, 20 Nanjing Road East; tel: 6321 6888; www.fairmont.com/peacehotel; $$
Victor's recreates the retro glamour of a 1930s European café, but its real draw is the freshly baked pastries and the floor-to-ceiling windows overlooking Nanjing Road.

Centre (492m/1,614ft, third-tallest) and Jinmao Tower (420m/1,377ft, tenth-tallest).

PARK 33

**2**

No.s 33–53 Waitan Yuan
former British Consulate

Suzhou Road South

Waibaidu Qiao

Suzhou Creek
(Wusong)

Yuanmingyuan Road

Peninsula
Shanghai

Renmin Yingxiong
Jinianbei
(Monument to the
People's Heroes)

HUANGPU
GONGYUAN
(HUANGPU PARK)

**1**

No.29 Guangda Yinhang
(Everbright Bank)

Beijing Road (East)

No.27 Luosifu
(House of Roosevelt)

Pu Vendmingyuan

No.26 Nongye Yinhang

No.24 Zhongguo
Gongshang Yinhang

No.23 Zhongguo Yinhang
(Bank of China)

Dianchi Road

**3**

No.20 Heping Fandian
(Fairmont Peace Hotel & Museum)
former Cathay Hotel

**4**

**1**

Nanjing Road East

No.16 Zhongguo
Zhaoshang Yinhang
(China Merchants Bank)
former Bank of Taiwan

No.15 Zhongguo Wai Hui
Jiao Yi Zhongxin
(Shanghai Gold Exchange)
former Russo-Asiatic Bank

Jiujiang Rd

No.14 former Bank
of Communications

Hankou Road

No.13 Laohaiguan
(Customs House)

**5**

No.12 Shanghai
Pudong Fazhan Yinhang
(Pudong Development Bank)

**6**

Metropole
Hotel

Fuzhou Road

No.9

former
Hamilton
House

No.17
& Company
former Russell

No.7
Bangkok Bank

No.6

No.5 Huaxie Bank
(former Nissin Kisen
Kaisha Shipping Bldg)

Central Jiangxi Road

Central Sichuan Road

China
Minsheng
Bank

No.3
Three on the Bund

**2**

No.2
Waldorf Astoria
(former Shanghai Club)

**7**

**3**

Waitan Xinhao Tai
(Gutzlaff Signal Tower)

**8**

No.1 former
McBain Building

Guangdong Rd

Waitan
Tunnel

No.1 Road East (Bund)

Zhongshan

Promenade

Waitan Canguang Sui Dao
(Bund Sightseeing Tunnel)

Chen Yi

No.19 Heping Huizhong Fandian
(Swatch Art Peace Hotel) former Palace Hotel

No.18 Waitan Shibahao (Bund 18)
former Chartered Bank Building

No.17 Youbang Baoxian Dasha
(American International Assurance AIA)
former North China Daily News

Huangpu

N

200 m / 220 yds

No.28 Shanghai Renmin
Guangbo Diantai
(People's Broadcasting Station)

Waitan Tunnel

## SOUTHERN BUND

For a dramatic contrast, turn your attention back to the Bund, where you can see what was the tallest structure in the city in the early 20th century: the stately Edwardian red-and-white-brick **Swatch Art Peace Hotel** (Heping Huizhong Fandian), originally the Palace Hotel, at No.19. Its ornate wood-panelled and gilt-edged lobby is worth a look, as is the small plaque outside the original Art Nouveau revolving doors commemorating the 1909 meeting here of the International Opium Commission.

To its left stands **Bund 18** (Waitan Shibahao), winner of a UNESCO award for the exemplary restoration of the former 1927 Chartered Bank of Australia, India and China. Today it's home to Mr & Mrs Bund, named by *Restaurant* magazine as one of the world's top 100 restaurants. The **AIA Building** (Youbang Baoxian Dasha) next door was built in 1923 and was originally the home of the *North China Daily News*.

Continue south along the promenade, heading towards the clock tower. To the tower's right at No.14 is the 1947 former Bank of Communications building, now the Shanghai Trade Union Bank – the last edifice to be completed on the Bund before the establishment of the PRC. Its stripped Gothic Art Deco design is unique among the mostly neoclassical Bund buildings.

### The Big Ching

Cross at the traffic lights back to the west side of the Bund and enter the **Customs House** ❺ (Laohaiguan; Mon–Fri 9am–5pm, lobby only), built in 1925. Its four-faced clock – "Big Ching" to the British in the old days – still chimes "the East is Red" every quarter-hour. A plaque to the right of the entrance commemorates the Communist employees of the Customs service who operated a clandestine radio here before the People's Liberation Army took the city in May 1949. Enter the lobby (during working hours) to see the lovely ceiling mosaics.

Next door at No. 12 is another Bund legend: the **Shanghai Pudong Development Bank** ❻ (Shanghai Pudong Fazhan Yinhang; Mon–Fri 9am–5pm, lobby only). When it was built in 1923 for the Hongkong and Shanghai Bank, the architect's instruction was to "dominate the Bund". Enter its magnificent marble lobby and admire the spectacular ceiling, where mosaic panels depict eight cities in which the bank had branches in 1923.

Continue south to the Bund's only Victorian edifice, **No. 6 The Bund** (Waitan Liu Hao), built in 1881. Directly next door is **No. 5 The Bund** (Waitan Wu Hao), built for the Nissin Kisen Kaisha Shipping Company in 1921. On the seventh floor is **M on the Bund**, see ⑪②, the fashionable restaurant that kickstarted the Bund's renaissance in 1999.

Just a few doors down at No. 2 is perhaps the most legendary of all the Bund buildings: the former Shanghai Club, now the **Waldorf Astoria Hotel** ❼ (Shanghai Waitan Hua'erdaofu Jiudian; tel: 6322 9988; www.hilton.com). The old boys who controlled Shanghai made many business and political decisions within its burnished wood-and-leather confines. To your left of the beautifully restored 1910 marble lobby (with original cage lift) is a faithful re-creation of the famous Long Bar. To the right, the **Salon de Ville**, see ⑪③, is a gorgeous setting for tea.

Exit and cross the Bund again to visit the 1908 **Gutzlaff Signal Tower** ❽ (Waitan Xinhao Tai, 1 Zhongshan No. 2 Road; tel: 6321 6542; daily 9am–11pm), which once announced weather conditions via nautical flags flown from its pinnacle.

**Above from far left:** ceiling details at the Peace Hotel and the Shanghai Pudong Development Bank; the Customs House with a typically flamboyant modern tower in the background.

---

## Food and Drink 🍴

### ② M ON THE BUND
20 Guangdong Road, 7th floor; tel: 6350 9988; www.m-restaurantgroup.com; daily 11.30am–2pm, 6pm–midnight; $$$
Award-winning M consistently tops the polls as Shanghai's best restaurant – it's a wonderful combination of smart but unfussy modern European cuisine, warm service and breathtaking Bund views.

### ③ SALON DE VILLE
Waldorf Astoria Shanghai, No. 2 The Bund; tel: 6322 9988; www.waldorfastoriashanghai.com; daily 4pm–1am; $$$
Shanghai's best traditional afternoon tea, in an old-school salon complete with live classical music and windows overlooking the Bund.

# BEHIND THE BUND

*The streets behind the Bund are some of the most thrillingly atmospheric in the city, from the historic buildings and high-end dining of "Missionary Row" to the gloriously unrestored banks and churches of the former International Settlement.*

---

**DISTANCE** 2km (1.2 miles)
**TIME** A half-day
**START** Peninsula Shanghai hotel
**END** M Glamour
**POINTS TO NOTE**
Take a taxi to the Peninsula Shanghai hotel to reach the starting point on Yuanmingyuan Road. Try to go on a Wednesday or Thursday to ensure access to buildings and museums open only during business hours. This tour can be combined with the Bund tour *(see p.28).*

---

**Name Game**
British surveyors laid out this part of the city in a logical grid pattern. They named the streets after China's cities and provinces: cities running east to west, provinces running north to south. The pinyin system is now used to transliterate Chinese street names, but the names themselves have remained unchanged since the 19th century.

The area behind the Bund was once home to old Shanghai's social institutions and recreational associations such as the YWCA, the Royal Asiatic Society, the Rotary Club and the Rowing Club. Neglected for decades, they have now been given a new lease of life as part of Waitanyuan, a "lifestyle zone" that incorporates shopping, fine dining and culture in and around the historic buildings, injecting new life into the neighbourhood.

## MISSIONARY ROW

From the Beijing Road entrance of the **Peninsula Shanghai ❶** (Ban Dao Fandian; tel: 2327 2888; www.peninsula.com), it's just a few steps west to the foot of Yuanmingyuan Road, old Shanghai's "Missionary Row". Before 1949, missionaries made up a significant percentage of China's foreign population, and Shanghai was the centre of the thriving enterprise. This stretch of buildings housed the offices of many missions.

Look carefully at the carved designs around the doorframe of the **YWCA Building ❷** (133 Yuanmingyuan Road): you can still make out the organisation's logo. The building's Chinese Art Deco design was created by Chinese-American architect Poy Gum Lee, and includes an interior with bright green and red tiles with the stylised character for "long life". Now unoccupied, the building was once home to the Shanghai branch of the Rotary Club and *The Chinese Recorder*, a missionary journal.

A few buildings along is the **Lyceum Building** (185 Yuanmingyuan Road), not a missionary building but a groundbreaking commercial one: built in 1937 by the Shanghai Land Investment Company, the building featured an attached warehouse, office space and ground-floor display windows.

A number of missions had their offices a few doors down at the **Missions Building** (169 Yuanmingyuan Road), including the American Bible Society, the China Council of the Presbyterian Church, the London Missionary Society, the National Bible Society of Scotland, the American Red Cross, and its main occupant, the National Christian Council.

The most striking building on the street is the "True Light" building at No. 209, with its dramatic Gothic Art Deco facade designed by prolific Shanghai-based Hungarian architect László Hudec in 1933. Officially known as the **China Baptist Publication Society Building**, the group printed Baptist publications, including the *True Light* journal, Sunday school lessons and Bible tracts.

At the north end of Yuanmingyuan Road, turn right to see the latest incarnation of the **Union Church** (Suzhou Road South), first established by the British on this location in 1886. Somewhat mysteriously destroyed by fire in 2007, it was reconstructed in time for the World Expo 2010 in Shanghai, but remains firmly shut, its exterior a favourite spot for brides-to-be to pose for photographs.

## AROUND SUZHOU CREEK

Take a look at what remains of the Shanghai Rowing Club across Suzhou Road before turning back and crossing the Zhapu Road Bridge to the **Shanghai Postal Museum** ❸ (Shanghai Youzheng Bowuguan; 250 Suzhou Road North; Wed, Thur, Sat, Sun 9am–5pm; free). Built in 1924 to serve as the main post office for both foreigners and Chinese, the building is still a functioning post office. The

Above from far left: looking north along the Bund and its riverside promenade; dragon boat racing on Suzhou Creek.

**Above:** Art Deco glamour at the Peninsula.

**Shanghai Speak**
The verb "Shanghaied" entered the English language during the 1870s to describe the act of drugging and kidnapping men in the sailors' bars behind the Bund to fill up ships' companies just before leaving port.

Postal Museum is accessed through an entrance at the northeast corner of the second floor. The information provided on the history of the Chinese postal service is interesting enough, but the real treasure is the astounding view of Shanghai from the museum's roof terrace.

As you stroll along the pedestrian path next to Suzhou Creek, pause and look back at Suzhou Road for a rare view of the buildings behind the Bund. It's a good vantage point to take in the **Capitol Building** (146 Huqiu Road), an Art Deco marvel of its day. The city's first air-conditioned theatre, it was constructed so that no columns obstructed the view to the movie screen. The interior was graced with thespian-themed murals and sculptures, and major Hollywood studios maintained offices here.

Just west of the Postal Museum, also facing the creek, is the sinuous Art Deco facade of **Embankment House**, built in 1932 by the fabled Sir Victor Sassoon. Originally boasting 194 flats, it was Shanghai's largest apartment building at the time.

### HUQIU ROAD

Cross back to Suzhou Road via the Sichuan Bridge, stopping at the midpoint for one of the city's best views, taking in Pudong, Hongkou and the buildings behind the Bund. Head east on Suzhou Road to Huqiu Road.

No. 128 is the rear of the True Light building, with a different look, a different name (the **Christian Literature Society Building**) and different occupants: this side housed missionary libraries as well as offices, including Hudec's own.

Continue south on Huqiu to the **Rockbund Art Museum** ④ (Shanghai Waitan Meishuguan; 20 Huqiu Road; Tue–Sun 10am–6pm; charge). Located in the elegant former Royal Asiatic Society building, it's another fine example of Shanghai Art Deco fusion, designed by British architect George L "Tug" Wilson. Rotating exhibitions of modern art are spread across its four floors.

### SOUTH TOWARDS FUZHOU ROAD

From here, take a detour southeast via Yuanmingyuan Road to the **Bund Tea Company**, see ⑪①, for tea and snacks; it's about two blocks south on Dianchi Road. Carry on to Central Sichuan Road and walk three blocks to the beautiful Beaux Arts Georgian **Guangdong Development Bank** (Guangdong Fazhang Yinhang) at No. 261, with its distinctive octagonal tower. The former Joint Savings Society Building, it was designed by László Hudec in 1926.

A block west stands the 1866 **Holy Trinity Cathedral** (219 Jiujiang Road), a classic Gothic Revival building built in eye-catching red brick, hence the Chinese name "Hong Miao" (Red Temple). Recent extensive renovations are complete, but no announcement has yet been made as to when it will finally be reopened to the public. Next to the church is the former Cathedral School for Boys, where JG Ballard, author of *Empire of the Sun*, attended primary school.

*Art Deco Highlights*

A block south on **Jiangxi Road, at the intersection of Fuzhou Road ❺**, rises a dramatic series of buildings – three Art Deco skyscrapers and one lower building in neoclassical style. The Metropole Hotel is the almost identical twin of Hamilton House, which in the 1930s housed offices, consulates and residences. Both were owned by Sir Victor Sassoon and were designed by Palmer & Turner. The lower building is the former Shanghai Municipal Council Chambers; the SMC ceased functioning after World War II and for most of the past half century this building has been used as offices of various Shanghai People's Government departments.

A short detour west on Fuzhou Road will bring you to a lovely 1924 red-brick Federalist-style building at No. 209 – the former Shanghai American Club, now empty.

**Shanghai Grandmother**, see ②, one block east on Fuzhou Road at Sichuan Road, serves deliciously authentic Shanghainese cuisine. Continue south on Sichuan Road to the next corner, 93 Guangdong Road, to see one of the true "Behind the Bund" gems: once home to the Metropolitan Life Insurance Co., it now houses government offices and a branch of **Minsheng Bank**. Its gorgeous stained-glass windows are best viewed from the serpentine marble lobby, so do go in if the building is open.

You're only a block from the Bund, so a post-walk tipple is definitely in order – and there is no better place than **M Glamour**, see ⑪③, at 20 Guangdong Road, with its trio of bars and spectacular views.

## Food and Drink

### ① BUND TEA COMPANY
100 Dianchi Road; tel: 6329 0989; daily 4–10pm; $
This historic British tea-trading company building houses a charming teahouse featuring an assortment of bespoke brews to taste and purchase, including green, black and flower teas.

### ② SHANGHAI GRANDMOTHER
70 Fuzhou Road (at Sichuan Road); tel: 6321 6613; daily 11.30am–2pm, 6–9.30pm; $
Authentic Shanghai-style home cooking, reputedly from a legendary grandmother's recipe files, in a pleasant, unstuffy setting. Signature dishes include tender *hongshaorou* (red-cooked pork) and classic *xiaolong bao* (steamed dumplings).

### ③ M GLAMOUR
No. 5 The Bund (entrance at 20 Guangdong Road); tel: 6350 9988; www.m-restaurantgroup.com; daily 5pm–2am; $$
Sister to M on the Bund, M Glamour has a cocktail bar, a wine bar and a champagne bar, plus a substantial food menu. The views of the Bund and the Shanghai skyline are stunning and the sophistication level is high.

# PEOPLE'S SQUARE

*The main square contains the very best of the modern city, from cutting-edge contemporary art to the imposing edifice of City Hall, with the wonders of old Shanghai tucked in among the shadows. Spend a day exploring here and you'll get close to the soul of the city.*

**DISTANCE** 2.5km (1.5 miles)
**TIME** A full day
**START** People's Park
**END** Park Hotel
**POINTS TO NOTE**
Take the metro to People's Square to reach the start (it's the main interchange, so you can take any number of lines) or ask a taxi to drop you at the park entrance on Nanjing Road. This museum-laden tour is ideal for art- and culture-lovers, and anyone on a rainy day.

People's Square is at the very heart of Shanghai, its exact centre and its showcase, home to world-class museums, a theatre, five-star hotels and the imposing City Hall in the middle of it all. Before it became a public space, this was the Shanghai Racecourse, so brazenly bourgeois and decadent that it had to be razed and paved over for proletarian Shanghai. Today, the square's buildings – each one an architectural achievement – symbolise the economic and cultural progress of modern Shanghai.

**Tunnel Vision**
The underground passage between the Urban Planning Centre and the Shanghai Museum is one of numerous bomb shelters built in the 1960s in the aftermath of the Sino-Soviet split, when the country lived in fear of a Soviet invasion.

## PEOPLE'S PARK

Enter **People's Park** ❶ (Renmin Gongyuan; 6am–6pm; free) from the north (Nanjing Road) or east (People's Square metro station). The building of modern Shanghai has encroached, reducing the size of the park, but it remains a lush oasis in the heart of the city with pretty tree-lined paths, a small lake and rock gardens. Come on Sundays to watch parents match-making for their grown children, clutching photos, posters and CVs in the hope of pairing them off.

### Art Centres
Follow the signs to the **Museum of Contemporary Art (MoCA)** ❷ (Shanghai Dangdai Yishu Guan; 231 Nanjing Road West, in People's Park; tel: 6327 9900; www.mocashanghai.org; daily 10am–9.30pm; charge). The city's first independent contemporary art museum features both international and Chinese contemporary works. Despite its relatively small size, MoCA shows some of the more cutting-edge, thought-provoking modern art in the city. Exhibitions, which

Above from far left:
Shanghai Art
Museum; t'ai chi in
People's Park.

change every two months, are on the first two floors of the three-storey glass structure, while a restaurant with an outdoor terrace overlooking the park is on the third.

Exit the park on Nanjing Road and head west through the imposing gates of the **Shanghai Art Museum** ❸ (Shanghai Meishuguan; 325 Nanjing Road West; tel: 6327 2829; www.sh-artmuseum.org.cn; daily 9am–5pm; charge), located in the neoclassical 1933 Shanghai Race Club building. Look for the "SRC" engraved over the building's entrance, and the horse heads on the ironwork banisters. Chinese art, both traditional and modern, is the focus of most of the exhibits. There are great views over People's Square from **Kathleen's 5**, see ⑪①, *p.39*, on the rooftop – a good spot for lunch or a drink.

Leaving the museum, walk south a block along Huangpi Road, where you can stop at **Wagas**, see ⑪②, *p.39*, in Central Plaza for a sandwich or coffee. Continue to People's Avenue and the **Shanghai Grand Theatre** (Shanghai Dajuyuan; 300 People's Avenue; tickets: 6372 3833; www.shgtheatre.com; tours Mon 9–11am; charge). Designed by French architect Jean-Marie Charpentier, the futuristic glass confection has flamboyantly upturned

Left: Shanghai Art Museum

eaves, mimicking a traditional Chinese roof. Dubbed the "Crystal Palace" by locals, the 1,800-seat theatre hosts a packed season of ballet, classical music and opera, some imported and some local. The Monday tours are a great way to get an insider's look at the theatre.

## SHANGHAI URBAN PLANNING CENTRE

Continue east along People's Avenue, past Shanghai City Hall (which will almost certainly interfere with your mobile phone reception) to the **Shanghai Urban Planning Centre ❹** (Shanghai Chengshi Guihua Guan;

100 People's Avenue; tel: 6372 2077; www.supec.org; Tue–Thur 9am–5pm, Fri–Sun 9am–6pm; charge, extra with audio guide) to make some sense of urban Shanghai. The museum's highlights are on the third floor: the remarkable 500 sq m (5,380 sq ft) scale model of Shanghai depicts every building over six storeys high, including ones as yet unbuilt. Also on this floor is the not-to-be-missed *Journey of Wonder in Shanghai*, a 360-degree movie that takes the audience on a bird's-eye flight across the city. For another excellent view, the top-floor café – which is almost always empty – has wonderful views across People's Square.

## SHANGHAI MUSEUM

From the Urban Planning Centre, find the underground passageway that will take you to the south side of People's Avenue and follow the signs to the **Shanghai Museum** ❺ (Shanghai Bowuguan; 201 People's Avenue; tel: 6372 3500; www.shanghaimuseum.net; daily 9am–5pm; free, charge for Acoustiguide rental plus deposit). Cross the landscaped plaza and pass the soaring musical fountain – full of kids trying to cool off in summer – to reach the distinctive round, granite building.

This is probably the best museum in the country. Shaped like a *ding* (a traditional cooking vessel), it focuses on the arts and crafts of China in its 11 permanent galleries, arranged thematically across four floors. Be sure to visit the Ancient Bronze Gallery, the Ancient Chinese Ceramic Gallery, which traces this born-in-China craft from the Neolithic Yellow River cultures to the Qing Dynasty. Other must-sees include the nation's largest collection of Chinese paintings in the Chinese Painting Gallery and the colourful Chinese Minorities Nationalities Gallery. Allow at least a couple of hours here.

### HIGHLIGHTS FROM THE GOLDEN AGE

Like a brand-new portrait set within an antique frame, the ultra-modern core of Shanghai is surrounded by the

legends that defined old Shanghai: its tallest building, best theatre and wildest entertainment. Leave the museum via the south entrance and cross busy Yan'an Road to the elegant neoclassical **Shanghai Concert Hall** (Shanghai Yinyueting). Built in 1930 as the Nanking Theatre, today it's home to the Shanghai Philharmonic Orchestra.

Head east to the intersection with Tibet Road, and to the wedding-cake building that dominates the corner: the legendary **Great World** (Da Shijie), controlled in the 1930s by Huang Jinrong ("Pockmarked Huang"), the head of the Concession's detective squad and a member of Shanghai's underworld Green Gang. In its heyday, the building was filled with entertainment of a

Above from far left: historic artefacts and artwork fill the Shanghai Museum in People's Square; the Shanghai Concert Hall; the bold exterior of the Urban Planning Centre.

---

### Food and Drink

**① KATHLEEN'S 5**
5th Floor, Shanghai Art Museum, 325 Nanjing Road West; tel: 6327 2221; www.kathleens5.com.cn; daily 11.30am–1pm; $$$
Perched atop the Shanghai Art Museum, Kathleen's 5 sits just under the old clock tower and offers spectacular views over People's Square from an outdoor terrace and glassed-in dining room. The restaurant serves continental cuisine, drinks and tea all day long.

**② WAGAS**
227 Huangpi Road (N); tel: 5375 2758; daily 7am–10pm; $$
This home-grown Shanghai brand is popular for its fresh, healthy menu of sandwiches, salads, pastas, home-made desserts and smoothies – plus free WiFi on tap. It's a good spot for a quick, tasty meal or to pick up a coffee to sip as you sightsee.

**Above:** a large-scale model of Shanghai on display at the Urban Planning Centre.

mostly unsavoury nature, an endless array of smoky gambling dens, dance halls and the infamous "staircase to nowhere" (where desperate souls could take the quick way out). Today, the Great World is locked up tight, awaiting a new lease of life.

Next door, the **Chinese YMCA** building, with its upturned eaves and ornate halls, is a beautiful example of the Sino-Western design fusion that is so distinctively Shanghai.

Walk back across Yan'an Road, pausing to admire the former **Grand Hotel** at No. 120, a grand edifice that is now a "Worker's Cultural Palace", a legacy of the 1950s when resources for-

merly reserved for the moneyed classes were made available to the new masters of New China – the working classes.

If you're hungry, head to mega mall **Raffles City**, see ⑪③, which dominates this block of Tibet Road and seems to be permanently packed with shoppers at any time of day. Head up to the sixth floor, where a food court offers a choice of Asian and Western delicacies.

Continue back to **Moore Church** ❻ (Mu'en Tang; 316 Tibet Road; services Sun 7.30am, 9am, 2pm, 7pm). The 1931 church, named after the Texas Methodist who donated funds for its construction, was built by innovative

## László Hudec, Shanghai's Master Architect

László Hudec (1893–1958) was already a chartered architect when, as a lieutenant in the Austro-Hungarian army, he was taken prisoner by the Russian army and sent to a Siberian prison camp. Hudec eventually escaped and made his way to Shanghai, where he found work with the American architectural firm RA Curry. There, he designed dozens of important buildings, including the American Club and the Normandie ISS Apartments. But his real masterpieces were created after 1925, when he set up his own firm. Inspired by the modernist architecture of New York, Hudec designed some of Shanghai's most innovative buildings, three of which are within a few metres of each other along Nanjing Road and Tibet Road: the Art Deco Grand Theatre cinema, the Park Hotel and the Moore Church.

architect László Hudec and includes a surprising undulating effect in the exterior brickwork. Used as a middle school throughout the Cultural Revolution, it was the first church in Shanghai to reopen in the late 1970s and the first to consecrate bishops.

Return north then west on Nanjing Road to the line of gracious old buildings that once defined progressive Shanghai. When the eight-storey **Pacific Hotel** (Jinmen Dajiudian, 108 Nanjing Road West) was built in 1924 as the Union Insurance Building, it was the tallest building in the city, and its bell tower was used by ships for navigation. Just west of the hotel is the **Shanghai Sports Club**, formerly the International YMCA (Chinese residents had to use the Chinese YMCA). Some of the remaining "Old Shanghailanders" remember attending afternoon tea dances in the second-floor ballroom; local residents continued this tradition until 2010,

when the ballroom was turned into an exhibition hall.

The next building down is the **Park Hotel** ❼ (Guoji Fandian; 170 Nanjing Road West), the 24-storey Hudec masterpiece that inspired architect IM Pei during his 1940s childhood. Built in 1934 for the Joint Savings Society, it was Shanghai's tallest and most advanced building until the 1980s. Sadly, little of the original Art Deco interior survives. Better to venture into the **Grand Theatre** cinema next door, also Hudec's handiwork, to see its lively Art Deco lobby.

Above from far left: "Zero Center Point" in the lobby of the Park Hotel; interior of the Grand Theatre.

Below: The Park Hotel.

## Food and Drink

③ **RAFFLES CITY**
268 Central Xizang Road; daily 10am–8pm; $
Raffles City is a Singapore brand, and its 6th floor mega food court is a Singapore-style one, with a huge array of stalls lining the perimeter. There are both Asian and western cuisines available here, from sushi to wontons, burgers to fresh juices.

# NANJING ROAD WEST

*Nanjing Road West is well known for its luxury shopping and latte sipping opportunities, but there's much more to be discovered here: this long street is surrounded by a rich mix of religious buildings, grand mansions and neighbourhood lanes.*

**DISTANCE** 5km (3 miles)
**TIME** A full day
**START** Junction of Nanjing Road and Taixing Road
**END** Hengshan Moller Villa
**POINTS TO NOTE**
Take the metro (line 2) to Nanjing Road West station, or a taxi to the start point. Avoid the weekend crowds. This walk is mostly outdoors, so save it for a dry day.

Nanjing Road's westernmost flank dominates the Jing An area. Much has changed since the time it was called Bubbling Well Road and a 1930s guidebook claimed it was "one of the seven most interesting streets in the world". Nowadays, the faded grandeur of its early 20th-century buildings yields to café society, where Shanghai's smart set flock to sip lattes and slurp on sundaes, before heading for the designer malls that form the bustling heart of this shopping district.

## LANE LIFE

At the intersection of Nanjing Road and Taixing Road, head south on the latter and through the black ironwork gates you see ahead of you, leaving the bustle behind as you enter a **Shanghai lane neighbourhood ❶** *(lilong)*. Stroll down the lanes between the *shikumen* (stone gate) houses, where neighbours chat on doorsteps and children play. Return the way you came, pausing to admire the profile of the 1934 Medhurst Building on the corner of Nanjing Road and Taixing Road.

Head west along the south side of Nanjing Road, where the latest, hippest brands entice with eye-catching window displays. About a block and a half down is Meilongzhen Restaurant (Lane 22, 1081 Nanjing Road West), one of the city's most famous Shanghainese eateries. Its reputation exceeds the fare, so eat only if you're starving. However, do admire the pink-brick mansion in which it's housed (the Chinese entrance is a later addition).

### Designer Malls

Cross Nanjing Road to the north side, where a row of designer malls converge: Westgate Mall, CITIC Square and Plaza 66, high-ceilinged, marble-floored edifices where Shanghai's well-heeled flock to Burberry, Cartier and Louis Vuitton. Enter Jiangning Road, and next door to Westgate Mall you'll see the lovely Streamline

Moderne **Majestic Theatre** with its round facade at No. 66, built in 1941 by Chinese architect Robert Fan.

### Jewish Legacy

Continuing north along Jiangning Road, turn left at the end of the block on to Beijing Road, then right on to Shaanxi Road North. Pass by Grace Church, built during World War II, and continue to the former **Ohel Rachel Synagogue ❷** (Youtai Jiao-tang; 500 North Shaanxi Road; closed to public). This grand Greek Revival temple was built in 1920 by Jacob Sassoon in memory of his wife, Rachel. The synagogue, facing Jerusalem, served as the spiritual home for the city's wealthy Sephardic Jewish community until 1952; see the portrait of Mao over the former Ark of the Covenant.

### PEI MANSION HOTEL

**Lynn**, see ⑪①, on Xikang Road, a block parallel to Shaanxi, serves excellent Shanghainese fare in modish

Above from far left:
Luis Vuitton flagship store at Plaza 66; a tie rack at Tony the Tailors; shoppers walk along pedestrianised Nanjing Road East, one of the main shopping districts in Shanghai.

**Shanghai's Synagogue**
Judaism is not one of Shanghai's five official religions (Protestantism, Catholicism, Islam, Taoism and Buddhism), so while the synagogue is sometimes opened up for Jewish community events, it cannot be used for religious worship.

---

## Food and Drink 🍴

### ① LYNN

99-1 Xikang Road; tel: 6247 0101; daily 11.30am–2pm, 6–10pm; $$
This chic restaurant serves up quality versions of Shanghainese classics in a stylish, upscale environment. The red-cooked pork and *xiaolongbao* are not to be missed.

**Above:** the interior of Hengshan Moller Villa.

surroundings. After lunch here, turn left on Xikang Road and then left into Nanyang Road. Past the Big Bamboo sports bar you'll find the gorgeous **Pei Mansion Hotel** ❸ (170 Nanyang Road), a Shanghai Art Deco gem built as the home of banker Pei Zuyi, whose nephew would become the renowned architect IM Pei. This is a lovely, quiet spot for a short break – take a seat in the pretty gazebo. If you have a drink at the restaurant you can explore the interior, which features a stunning staircase spiralling towards a glass dome, and Chinese motifs throughout.

### SHANGHAI EXHIBITION CENTRE

Exit the Pei Mansion and head west to Tongren Road to find the former **Woo House** at No. 33. Built by László Hudec in 1938 as a private home for a dyeworks magnate, its distinctive architecture, with a round tower, is enhanced by green glazed tiles on the exterior. The interior was briefly open to the public as a restaurant, but now what was once one of the most luxurious residences in the city is closed and awaiting its next act.

Continue two blocks south on Tongren Road to its intersection with Nanjing Road West, where you'll find the landmark **Shanghai Exhibition Centre** ❹ (Shanghai Zhanlan Zhongxin; 1000 Central Yan'an Road, entrance also on Nanjing Road; daily

9am–5pm; free). The "Russian wedding cake" was built during the 1950s as an expression of common cause between China and its long-time supporter the Soviet Union. The complex sits on what was, until the revolution, the sprawling estate of Silas Hardoon, who arrived in Shanghai in the 1870s and died its richest resident in 1930.

Directly across the street is the John Portman & Associates-designed **Shanghai Centre** (Shanghai Shangcheng; 1376 Nanjing Road West; tel: 6279 8600; www.shanghaicentre.com). The city's first international residential, business and hotel complex (opened in 1989) is popular with expatriates, and boasts the conveniences of groceries, shopping, a clinic, tennis courts, the Portman Ritz-Carlton and a clutch of restaurants. For lunch, homegrown franchises **Element Fresh**, see ⑪②, and **Baker & Spice**, see ⑪③, are both good options. The complex also includes the Shanghai Centre Theatre, home of the renowned Shanghai Acrobatic Troupe – well worth a visit.

### JING AN TEMPLE AND PARK

Two blocks west is the garish, newly constructed **Jing An Temple** ❺ (Jingan Si). Now more a destination for shoppers than the devout, it was known in pre-1949 Shanghai as Bubbling Well Temple, after the effervescent well in the middle of Nanjing Road, which was removed in the 1970s. There has been a temple on this site for hundreds of years, but almost nothing from previous versions survived the 2002 construction of the present structure. Especially unsightly is the lion-topped gilded column in front of the temple, which is meant to recreate a much more pleasantly proportioned column that didn't survive the Cultural Revolution.

Now cross to the south side of Nanjing Road and enter **Jing An Park** ❻ (Jingan Gongyuan; 1649 Nanjing Road West; free, but charge for entrance to some sites within the park). Elderly men sit on benches shaded by the enormous plane trees that lined the entrance to what was once the cemetery attached to the Bubbling Well Temple.

Leave Jing'an Park by the Huashan Road exit and head west along Yan'an Road to the **Municipal Children's Palace** ❼ (Shi Shaonian Gong; 64 Central Yan'an Road; tel: 6248 1850; free) where children receive instruction in the performing arts, calligraphy and (more recently) computers. Originally built in 1924 as a residence for the Kadoorie family (current owners of the Peninsula Shanghai), it was nicknamed "Marble Hall" because of the extensive use of that stone throughout. Try to talk your way in for a look around and hope that the guards are in a good mood.

## MOLLER VILLA

Exit on Yan'an Road and take a taxi to your final stop: a fairytale castle. At the intersection of Shaanxi Road, you'll see the steeples and spires of the **Hengshan Moller Villa** ❽ (Hengshan Male Biehu; 30 Shaanxi Road South; tel: 6247 8881; www.mollervilla.com), a boutique hotel named after its original owner, Swedish shipping magnate Eric Moller. Wander the grounds to get a look at the house from different perspectives, and then enter the hotel: the sheer grandeur of the place – rich wood panelling, crystal chandeliers – brings alive the glamour of old Shanghai.

**House of Horror**
The story goes that a fortune teller told Hengshan Moller Villa owner Eric Moller that ill fortune would befall him if he ever finished the house, so he kept adding bits for years. When he finally finished the house in 1949, he died in a plane crash.

### Food and Drink 🍴

**② ELEMENT FRESH**
Shanghai Centre, 1376 Nanjing Road West; tel: 6385 8752; www.elementfresh.com; daily 7am–11pm; $$
This light-filled California-style eatery has terrace seating overlooking Nanjing Road. Good options include pastas, wraps, sandwiches and smoothies.

**③ BAKER & SPICE**
Shanghai Centre, 1376 Nanjing Road West; tel: 5404 2733; daily 7am–9pm; $$
A great spot for a break on Nanjing Road – both because of its outdoor terrace seating and its tempting array of freshly baked goods. The cupcakes and tarts are highly recommended.

# THE OLD CHINESE CITY

*A walk through old China – and Shanghai's 21st-century interpretation of old China – takes you past the area's ancient temples, brash bazaars and air-conditioned malls, before finding some inner peace in the classical surroundings of Yu Garden.*

**DISTANCE** 2km (1.2 miles)
**TIME** A half-day
**START** Yu Yuan metro station
**END** Confucius Temple
**POINTS TO NOTE**
Take the metro (line 10) to Yu Yuan station and leave by Exit 1, or take a taxi to Fuyou Road/Henan Road. Go on a weekday morning to avoid the worst of the crowds – particularly at Yu Garden. It's a good tour for kids, but keep an eye on them among the crowds.

When the British arrived in Shanghai in 1842 they found a thriving walled city of perhaps 200,000 people, which had evolved from a small fishing settlement that had been established here some 800 years. Earlier parts of today's "Old City" may be a theme-park version of Ming China, but there's still some of the traditional town in the packed lanes, crowded markets and classical garden, making it a fascinating contrast to the ultra-modern glass-and-steel metropolis that surrounds it.

**Sleep Walking**
It's not uncommon to see Shanghainese out walking in their local neighbourhood dressed in pyjamas. The lanes, and therefore the local neighbourhood, are considered to be an extension of their personal living space.

## FUYOU ROAD AND AROUND

Enter Fuyou Road from Henan Road. Your first hint that you're in the Old City is a ramshackle row of 19th-century shops at 384–392 Fuyou Road – look up to see the original wooden window hinges on the second floor. Just ahead is the **Fuyou Road Mosque ❶** (Fuyou Lu Qingzhensi; 378 Fuyou Road; daily 6am–7pm; free), established in 1853 by Muslim traders whose ancestors had been active in Chinese commerce for a millennium. The mosque has three main halls: the original core; the main prayer hall, built in 1897; and the Art Deco-influenced entrance building, erected in 1936. Shanghai's first Islamic school was once located within the complex, and the Muslim Business Society, established in 1911, met here as well.

Back on Fuyou Road, head south on to Houjia Road and east on to Chen Xiangge Alley, where you'll soon spot the bright mustard walls of the **Chenxiangge Nunnery ❷** (Chenxiangge; 29 Chenxiangge Alley; daily 7am–5pm, 1st and 15th days of the lunar calendar 5.30am–4pm; charge). Filial son Pan Yunduan established this temple in 1600 in honour of his mother, some 30 years after creating Yu Garden for his father. Briefly a factory during the Cultural Revolution, the temple was restored in 1994. A new gilded Buddha and its 384 exquisitely sculpted *luohan* (Buddhist saints) are highlights, but the real stars are the nuns, whose chanting can be heard throughout the day.

Continue down Chenxiangge Alley, turn left and then re-enter Fuyou Road, heading east (to the right). Soon you'll see the **Fuyou Road Merchandise Mart** (Fuyou Lu Shichang; daily 8am–5pm) and **Fumin Street Smallware Market** (Fumin Shang Sha; daily 8am–5pm). China is the world's factory, and pretty much *everything* can be found here at discounted prices.

## TEMPLE OF THE CITY GOD

Exit the shops and head south on Anren Street, a quiet historic lane where you might find women shelling peas and children playing hide-and-seek. At the Fangbang Road intersection, turn right and head for the **Temple of the City God ❸** (Chenghuang Miao; 249 Central Fangbang Road; daily 8.30am–4.30pm; charge). Dedicated to the gods that protect Shanghai, this was historically the town hub. This is a post-Cultural Revolution

restoration of the 1726 building, constructed in honour of the legendary general Huo Guang. Look out for the Taoist deities wearing what look like bowler hats.

## DRAGON GATE MALL

Exit the temple the way you entered, and head east (left) on Fangbang Road. **Dragon Gate Mall** on your right (168 Central Fangbang Road; daily 10am–9pm) is a sprawling vision of the "new Old City", with H&M, Marks & Spencer and air-conditioned cafés. But we're heading for the *old* Old City. Follow Fangbang Road for about

Above from far left: statues at the Temple of the City God; the Lantern Festival at Yu Garden.

a block, where it turns into a pedestrian lane lined with 19th-century buildings. Here you'll find everything from lucky underwear shops to apothecaries, pickle specialists, rice wine purveyors, vendors with carts on the sidewalk shouting out bargains, loud music and lots of *renao* – Shanghai buzz.

For some authentic street food, turn right on to **Sipailou Road**, see ⑪①, marked by a *pailou* (traditional Chinese archway) and lined with the city's most delicious street food.

**China on a Plate**
The Huxinting Teahouse is popularly believed to be the model for Willow Pattern plates, first created by Josiah Spode in 1790 during the heyday of the China trade and based on an original pattern called the Mandarin.

## MING-STYLE BAZAAR

Head back to Fangbang Road and retrace your steps past the City God Temple to enter the atmospheric **Yu Garden Bazaar** ❹ (Yu Yuan Shangcheng; Central Fangbang Road, Entrance No. 6; daily 7am–late) on your right.

This bold, brash bazaar with new Ming-style buildings is a cacophony of shops, street performers, sedan-chair rides and people, people, people. Follow the signs to the **Huxinting Teahouse** ❺ (Huxinting Chashe; daily 7am–7pm), see ⑪②, set on a lake and accessed by the zigzag Bridge of Nine Turnings (because evil spirits can't turn corners). The five-sided teahouse is surprisingly quiet: most people prefer to gaze from the outside. It's a rare experience to sip delicate Chinese tea from a traditional Yixing teacup on

the second floor, with views of the willow trees.

*Yu Garden*
Complete your journey across the Bridge of Nine Turnings and buy a ticket for **Yu Garden** ❻ (Yu Yuan; opposite Huxinting Teahouse; daily 8.30am–5.30pm; charge). This lovely Jiangnan-style classical garden was built in 1577 by Ming official Pan Yunduan for his father in his old age ("*yu*" means peace and comfort).

The 2-hectare (5-acre) walled garden creates a microcosm of the universe and offers ingenious views, with its 30 pavilions connected by bridges and walkways crossing fish-ponds and rockeries. Highlights of the garden include the Grand Rockery (Dajiashan), a 2,000-tonne, 14m (46ft) sculpture of pale yellow rocks; and the Exquisite Jade Rock (Yu Ling Long).

The gardens' exit brings you back to the main plaza. Near the Bridge of Nine Turnings, find the entrance to the legendary **Nanxiang Dumplings** (Nanxiang Xiaolongbao), see ⑪③, and head up to the third floor for the delicious *xiao-longbao* (bite-sized dumplings filled with pork and scalding soup), sweet rice "pigeon-egg" dumplings, shortcakes and sesame paste-filled dumplings.

## SHANGHAI OLD STREET

Leave the bazaar the way you came and continue west on Central Fang-

Above from far left:
Huxinting Teahouse;
Grand Rockery, Yu
Garden; prayers
written on small
pieces of paper hang
from a tree at the
Confucius Temple.

bang Road, also known as **Shanghai Old Street**. The shops here sell Chinese-themed souvenirs: purple clay Yixing teapots, Chinese crafts, tea blends and Shanghai "calendar girl" posters. Admire the collection of Old Shanghai memorabilia over an atmospheric cup of tea at the **Old Shanghai Teahouse** (Lao Shanghai Chaguan), see 🍴④.

Continue west along Shanghai Old Street and then left (south) on Henan Road. Cross over busy Fuxing East Road to reach the **Peach Orchard Mosque** (Xiaotaoyuan Qingzhensi; 52 Xiaotaoyuan Road; daily 8am–7pm; free). This working mosque, with its distinctive green domes, was built in 1917 and renovated in 1925, but its mix of Middle Eastern, Chinese and Western architecture has a surprisingly contemporary feel.

## CONFUCIUS TEMPLE

Continue south on Henan Road, then right on to Wen Miao Road to the **Confucius Temple ❼** (Wen Miao; 215 Wen Miao Road; daily 9am–4.30pm; charge), where anxious students and their parents pray for good exam results by inscribing their entreaties on red paper and hanging them near the temple entrance. First established in the 18th century, the current temple dates from 1855. Of note are the God of Literature

Pavilion (Kui Xing) with its Chinese arched roof, and the Respecting Classics Tower (Zunjing Ta), a collection of Chinese classics that once served as the Kuomintang state library – and the headquarters for the Shanghai branch of the Small Swords Society during the Taiping Rebellion. A book market is held here on Sundays.

## Food and Drink

### ① SIPAILOU FOOD STREET
Off Central Fangbang East Road, between Gangu Street and Zhonghua Road; daily 8am–9pm; $
Outdoor stalls and simple cafés line this street offering everything from hand-pulled noodles and dumplings to quail egg omelettes, kebabs, tandoor bread and fruit. Come hungry so you can try a few things.

### ② HUXINTING TEAHOUSE
Yuyuan Bazaar, opposite Yu Garden; tel: 6373 6950; daily 7am–7pm; $
A classic "Old China" teahouse offering a variety of teas as well as snacks. Tables upstairs offer beautiful views of the treetops within Yu Garden. The tea is more expensive than elsewhere – but then again, few teahouses have this much history or atmosphere.

### ③ NANXIANG DUMPLINGS
Yu Garden Bazaar; tel: 6335 4206; daily 7am–8pm; $$
The restaurant's signature xiaolongbao (dumplings filled with pork, crab meat and a scalding soup) are top-notch. Reserve ahead so you can enjoy the dumplings in the third-floor restaurant.

### ④ OLD SHANGHAI TEAHOUSE
385 Central Fangbang Road; tel: 5382 1202; daily 9am–6pm; $$
This is a nostalgic slice of old Shanghai. The owner's Shanghai memorabilia is on display, and his qipao (cheongsam) collection is especially notable. The menu includes a wide range of teas and coffees.

# XINTIANDI

*A stroll through the rapidly changing neighbourhoods around Xintiandi's shopping and dining enclave takes you from the birthplace of the Chinese Communist Party to the heart of the city's consumer culture.*

---

**DISTANCE** 2km (1.2 miles)
**TIME** A half-day
**START** Wanshang Bird and Flower Market, Tibet Road
**END** Shikumen Open House Museum
**POINTS TO NOTE**
Take the metro (line 10) to Laoximen station and head to the starting point. Alternatively, take a taxi to Tibet Road/Fuxing Road. This is a good tour if you have children in tow.

---

**New Paradise**
Xintiandi, meaning "new paradise", comes from a song that was popular in old Shanghai. The song was about the city's legendary nightlife, and for older residents its name still evokes a sense of glamour.

Until recently, Xintiandi was just one of many Shanghai *lilongs*, or lane neighbourhoods. Its fortunes altered in 1999 when a developer, unable to build above the birthplace of the Communist Party next door, decided to retain the *lilong* within an upscale shopping and dining enclave. This novel gentrification project, unprecedented in China, became a nationwide sensation.

## OLD XINTIANDI

Despite the five-star luxury being constructed all around, much in the area is unchanged, including the lane neighbourhoods, the streetside eateries and the **Wanshang Bird and Flower Market ❶** (Wanshang Huaniao Shichang; 417 Tibet Road; daily 7am–7pm). During the summer cricket season, an entire section of the market is devoted to the insects, their paraphernalia and cricket fights. Songbirds are in another section, while the rest of the market is filled with more traditional pets: puppies, kittens, rabbits, hamsters, turtles and fish.

Cross Tibet Road and walk through the archway to the **Dongtai Road Antiques Market ❷** (Dongtai Lu Shichang; daily 10am–4pm), a mostly outdoor market covering more than two blocks, with 100 booths and two-storey shophouses with a mix of serious antiques and kitsch.

Turn left on to Dongtai Road. At the next intersection, turn right on Zizhong Road, then left on to Ji'an Road to soak up some genuine lane neighbourhood atmosphere. On the southwest corner of Ji'an Road and Fuxing Road, you may see paper models of fully furnished houses for sale. These are burned at funerals to ensure that one's ancestors are comfortable in the afterlife.

On the east side of the street, the **Fa Zang Temple** ❸ (Fa Zang Si; 271 Ji'an Road; daily 7am–4pm; charge), built in 1932, is probably the only Chinese Buddhist temple anywhere that incorporates Western architectural elements in its design.

## NEW XINTIANDI

Return to Fuxing Road and turn left, then right on to Ji'nan Road. At Hubin Road, turn left. On your right is One Corporate Avenue, with luxury car dealerships – this was a lane neighbourhood just a decade ago.

Turn left on to Huangpi Road, then right on to Xinye Road to reach the **Site of the First National Congress of the Communist Party of China** ❹ (Zhonggong Yida Huizhi; 76 Xingye Road; daily 9am–4pm; free). It was here, at No. 106, that the Chinese Communist Party was formed in 1921. Upstairs, the history of the CCP (according to the CCP) is recounted; the table around which the 13 delegates sat, including a young Mao Zedong, is set with 13 stools and teacups.

From the museum exit, return to Xinye Road to the entrance to **Xintiandi** ❺, the city's most popular shopping, dining and entertainment centre in the unique setting of a lane neighbourhood. On your right, the **Shikumen Open House Museum** ❻ (Wulixiang Bowuguan; Lane 181 Taicang Road, House 25; Sun–Thur

10.30am–10.30pm, Fri–Sat 11am–11pm; charge) recreates the interior of an authentic lane house. It's a fitting memorial to the houses demolished to create Xintiandi. Finish with lunch at **Crystal Jade**, see ⓘ①, or **Din Tai Fung**, see ⓘ②, both local favourites.

## Food and Drink 🍽

### ① CRYSTAL JADE

2/F, Nos. 6–7 South Block Xintiandi, Lane 123, Xingye Road; tel: 6385 8752; daily 11am–11pm; $$
Sleek decor, and top-notch dim sum and cuisine from across China. Favourites include *dan dan mian* – spicy Sichuan noodles with a chilli and peanut sauce; and *hong shao rou*, a Shanghainese pork dish. Reserve in advance.

### ② DIN TAI FUNG

2/F, No. 6 South Block Xintiandi, Lane 123, Xingye Road; tel: 6385 8378; Mon–Thur 11am–midnight, Sat–Sun 11am–1am; $$
The house special is Shanghai's signature dumpling, *xiaolong bao*, steamed dumplings filled with pork, ginger, garlic and a scalding broth. The *New York Times* hailed the original in Taiwan one of the world's 10 best restaurants.

# 7

# THE FORMER FRENCH CONCESSION

*Take a walk among the parks, mansions and mysteries of the western part of the former French Concession, where many historic homes are being transformed into hip restaurants, cafés, boutiques and music venues.*

**DISTANCE** 6km (3.7 miles)
**TIME** A full day
**START** Fuxing Park, junction of Chengdu Road and Central Fuxing Road
**END** French Consul's Residence, Central Huaihai Road
**POINTS TO NOTE**
Take the metro to Xintiandi station and walk west on Fuxing Road to the starting point. Alternatively, catch a taxi to the starting point.

**Historic Shanghai**
Shanghai's historic preservation group, Historic Shanghai (info@historic-shanghai.com), leads a monthly walking tour of the former French Concession. Led by Chinese-speaking historians and sinologists, the tours take you into homes, courtyards and hidden lanes to meet the locals and reveal layers of Shanghai's fascinating history.

In old Shanghai, it was said that the British would teach you how to do business but the French would teach you how to live. It's a maxim that still holds true, as the old villas and lane houses of the former French Concession are transformed into hip shopping, dining and entertainment enclaves.

## FUXING PARK

Originally a military drill field and subsequently laid out in 1907 as a public park (called the "French Park" by most locals), **Fuxing Park** ❶ (Fuxing Gongyuan; junction of Central Fuxing Road and Chengdu Road; daily 6am–6pm; free) still retains its European landscaping. A well-executed statue of Karl Marx and Friedrich Engels, added in the 1990s, beams down benevolently on the carnival of Chinese martial arts, synchronised exercise and ballroom dancing that can be found here every morning. An amusement park makes this a good stop for families.

Exit the park on to Gaolan Road and head south on Sinan Road to the **Former Residence of Sun Yat-sen** ❷ (Sun Zhongshan Guju; 7 Xiangshan Road; daily 9am–4.30pm; charge), celebrated as the father of the country on both sides of the Taiwan Strait. Sun's Kuomintang Party was established in 1905 with the aim of replacing the Qing Dynasty with democratic leadership, finally succeeding in 1911. He lived here with his wife, Soong Ching Ling, from 1918 to 1924. Inside the well-preserved house with its plush carpets and blackwood furniture, keep an eye out for Sun's map planning the Northern Expedition and a 1924 photo of Sun and Soong beside the first aeroplane in China.

The **Former Residence of Zhou Enlai ❸** (Zhou Enlai Guju; 73 Sinan Road; daily 9.30am–4pm; charge) is further south. The much beloved Premier and Foreign Minister of the People's Republic lived here in 1946 as head of the Communist Party mission during peace talks with Chiang Kai-shek's Nationalist government. The Spanish-style villa is furnished as it was in those heady days; an exhibition documenting Zhou's life is displayed in a separate building.

## RUIJIN GUESTHOUSE

Continue south along Sinan Road to Taikang Road and **Tianzifang**, a warren of lanes filled with galleries, boutiques, restaurants and shops. One of the best is photographer Erh Dong-qiang's gallery, showcasing photographs of China's Western architecture.

Exit Tianzifang at Central Jianguo Road, turn left, and then right on to Ruijin No. 2 Road to the sprawling lawns and grand manor houses of the **Ruijin Guesthouse ❹** (Ruijin Bing-guan; 118 Ruijin No. 2 Road). HE Morriss Jr, son of the *North China*

Above from far left: Fuxing Park life in Shanghai: ballroom dancing; chorus singing.

### Sinan Mansions
Directly south of Fuxing Park, several of this cluster of old French and British villas have been renovated to restore their original ambience. The complex features a series of restaurants and shops linked by outdoor piazzas.

*Daily News* owner, built the estate with its four villas in 1928. Many buildings have been added on the grounds, but the originals remain: climb the magnificent staircase to the landing in Building No. 1 to see an intricate Chinese screen with "foo dogs"; enter Building No. 3 to see the brilliant hues of a stained-glass window depicting a tiger in the jungle, the only surviving stained glass from the Siccawei Orphanage workshop, the rest having been lost during the Cultural Revolution.

Exit the guesthouse grounds on to Maoming Road, on the other side of which is the futuristic oval structure of the **Shanghai Culture Square** (Wenhua Guangchang), opened in 2011 after several years construction.

### SASSOON'S SHANGHAI

Head north on Maoming Road to the shopping hub of Central Huaihai Road. Here, amid the buzz of neon, block-long adverts and superscale shops, is a clutch of genteel old buildings, including property mogul Victor Sassoon's 1932 **Cathay Cinema** (Guotai Dianyingyuan; 870 Central Huaihai Road), an Art Deco classic that, then and now, screens Hollywood blockbusters and Chinese films.

Continue north on Maoming Road and enter the **Okura Garden Hotel** ❺ (Huayuan Fandian; 58 Maoming Road South) by the road entrance, if it's open. This New Baroque beauty is

the former Cercle Sportif Français – the French Club. Explore the original lobby with its glittering gold mosaics and polished marble columns, and head up the dramatic stairway. The original Grecian nudes still top the columns, and the ballroom's stunning stained-glass skylight remains intact. It is one of the earliest manifestations of Art Deco in Shanghai. The 20 lawn tennis courts are now gone, but the grounds are a lovely spot for a stroll.

Cross Maoming Road to the historic **Jinjiang Hotel** (Lao Jinjiang Fandian), built by Sir Victor Sassoon in 1928 as Cathay Mansions. He soon added the Art Deco Grosvenor House (luxury apartments today) and the low-rise Grosvenor Gardens, now offices. In 1972, US President Richard Nixon and China's Foreign Minister Zhou Enlai signed the Shanghai Communiqué at the Jinjiang, the first step towards normalising US–China relations after decades of enmity.

The **Lyceum Theatre** (Lanxin Daxiyuan) is a few steps north, at the corner of Changle Road. Built in 1930 as the home of the Shanghai Amateur Dramatic Club, legendary ballerina Margot Fonteyn performed here as a girl.

### CATHEDRALS AND CONSERVATORIES

Now head west on Changle Road, turning left on Shaanxi Road and then right on Xinle Road. After a block of supremely hip fashion boutiques, you'll see the sapphire-hued onion domes of the former **Cathedral of the Holy Mother of God**. Inspired by the Cathedral of the Saviour in Moscow, this 1931 Russian Orthodox church is now an exhibition space.

Continue to Donghu Road and turn left, passing the Donghu Hotel, a generous gift to Shanghai mafia chief Du Yuesheng in 1937 from a grateful disciple. Continue south and cross Central Huaihai Road to Fenyang Road. On your right will be the **Shanghai Conservatory of Music** (Shanghai Yinyue Xueyuan; 20 Fenyang Road; open daily), one of China's premier conservatories and the location of a pair of historic buildings. Refer to the map at the entrance to find Building No. 2, the former Jewish Club, and the Experts Building, formerly the Shanghai branch of the Betar, a revisionist Zionist organisation. Across Fenyang Road is **Madison Restaurant**, see ①①, a great lunch stop.

## SHANGHAI ARTS AND CRAFTS MUSEUM

Proceed south on Fenyang Road, crossing Fuxing Road, and enter the **Shanghai Arts and Crafts Museum** ❻ (Shanghai Gongyi Meishuguan; 79 Fenyang Road; daily 9am–4.30pm; charge) on your left. Set in lush grounds, this grand whitewashed mansion, its curved facade reminis-

cent of the US White House, was designed by László Hudec in 1905 for the director of the French Compagnie des Tramways and was later the home of New Shanghai's first mayor, Chen Yi. The museum's gorgeous interior houses an eclectic collection of dying crafts including wood, ivory and jade carving, silk embroidery, needlepoint and dough modelling.

### ELEGANT VILLAS

Head west on Dongping Road to **Sasha's** (Shasha), see ①②. Built in 1921 by Spanish architect Abelardo Lafuente, the mansion was the home of TV Soong of the powerful Soong family, said to be the richest man in the world. The villa next door was the home of TV's sister, Soong Mei-ling, wife of Nationalist China's president, Chiang Kai-shek. Adjacent to this was the

## Food and Drink

**① MADISON RESTAURANT**
No. 3 Fenyang Road, Building 2, 1F; tel: 6473 0136; daily 11am–11pm; $$
Innovative chef Austin Hu creates New American cuisine with distinctly Shanghai flavours, using locally sourced in-season ingredients from artisan and boutique producers.

**② SASHA'S**
11 Dongping Road, House No. 11; tel: 6474 6166; daily 11am–11pm; $$$
Continental cuisine in the former home of TV Soong, said to have once been the richest man in the world. The elegant second floor, with its wooden floors, high ceilings and fireplace, is the setting for Sasha's gourmet dishes.

home of another sister, Soong Ai-ling, married to HH Kung, head of the Bank of China. Only Soong Ching-ling, the widow of the Republic of China's first president, Sun Yat-sen, lived apart.

From Sasha's, turn left on to Hengshan Road. A five-minute walk will take you to the ivy-covered **International Community Church** (Guojie Jiaotang; 53 Hengshan Road; English services Sun 2pm, 4pm). Founded by a group of Americans in 1925, this Gothic Revival Protestant church has hosted celebrities from US presidents to Bishop Desmond Tutu.

The distinctive red-brick building across the street is the former **Shanghai American School** (Lao Meiguo Xuexiao), designed by American architect Henry Murphy to resemble Independence Hall in Philadelphia and opened at this location in 1923.

Continue along Hengshan Road and turn right at Gao'an Road. Enter Lane 18 to the **Xuhui Children's Palace** (Xuhuiqu Shaoniangong; 9am–4pm daily). Built in the latest Streamline Moderne style in 1939 for Rong Desheng, a member of a powerful industrialist family, the mansion is today a "children's palace" for after-school and weekend activities.

Walk straight out of the gate down the lane and exit on to Kangping Road. One block to your left is the modest ten-storey apartment building that was basketball star Yao Ming's childhood home. Just past Wanping Road

is the Shanghai headquarters of the Communist Party of China. There's no sign, but the soldiers at attention with bayoneted rifles are a sure tip-off – keep your camera in your bag.

## HENGHSAN PARK AND SOON CHING LING'S RESIDENCE

Return to Wanping Road and head south to visit pretty **Hengshan Park** (Hengshan Gongyuan; daily 6am–6pm; free). Formerly Pétain Park, after Vichy collaborator Marshal Pétain, it was laid out by the French in 1935, and 75 years' worth of lush greenery lends it a near-tropical feel. Beginning at dawn, the park buzzes with t'ai chi practitioners, old men getting haircuts, ballroom dancers and gossiping grandmas.

Retrace your steps along Wanping Road and continue north to Huaihai Road. Head west (left) until you reach **Soong Ching Ling's Former Residence ❼** (Song Qingling Guju; 1843 Central Huaihai Road; daily 9am–4.30pm, charge). Sun Yat-sen's young widow lived here from 1948 until she moved to Beijing in 1963, and the house stands as a monument to her and to the Communist Party to which she remained loyal despite her family's leadership roles in the opposing Kuomintang government. Visitors can see her bedroom suite – the furniture was a wedding present from her parents in 1915 – plus the living and dining rooms, with photographs of the dignitaries she entertained there, from Mao to Nehru. A modern building documents the extraordinary Soong clan in letters and artefacts, and in the garage sit two ebony limousines: a 1952 Jim, a gift from Stalin, and her own Chinese-made Red Flag.

Directly across the street are the beautiful **Normandie Apartments** (Wukang Dalou), a local landmark that dominates the north side of the street. Strongly reminiscent of Manhattan's Flatiron building, the Italianate structure was designed by László Hudec in 1924 for the Inter-savin Society (ISS), and named for the great ocean liner, the *Normandie*, from which it gets its shape.

## AROUND WUKANG ROAD

Cross Huaihai at the "prow" of the Normandie and head northeast on Wukang Road to the **Wukang Road Tourist Information Centre** (393 Wukang Road; tel: 6433 5000; daily 9am–5pm). The centre features scale models of the neighborhood's historic buildings, allowing you to see them from angles that would not otherwise be possible. About a block further, on your left, are the chic cafés and restaurants of **Ferguson Lane**, see ⑪③, a refurbished old factory.

Continue on Wukang Road and turn right on to Hunan Road, then left

on to Central Huaihai Road, at the **Shanghai Library** (Shanghai Tushu-guan; 1555 Central Huaihai Road; tel: 6445 5555; daily 8.30am–8.30pm). This spacious, light-filled facility, Asia's largest, houses collections of rare Chinese books, the Chinese Cultural Celebrities Manuscript Library and a genealogy section. Of particular note is a rare 8,000-volume Ming Dynasty edition of the *Taoist Scriptures*.

Exit the library and turn right on Huaihai Road. Next door, at 1517, is the Japanese Consul's residence, built for the northern warlord Duan Qi Rui around 1920. The US Consulate-General is at 1469 Huaihai Road, a neoclassical mansion built in the early part of the 20th century for prominent Chinese entrepreneur and Qing government minister Shang Shu. Across Ulumugi Road is the French Consul General's residence, 1431 Huaihai, built in 1921 for the French Basset family. It's closed to the public, but you can spot the lovely sunflower tiles just below the eaves over the high walls.

**Above from far left:**
Shanghai Arts and Crafts Museum; sculpture outside Coffee Tree on Ferguson Lane; the Shanghai Library.

**Jiashan Market**
On Jiashan Road, a few blocks south of Huaihai Road, Jiashan Market is a farmer's market held by expat boutique food producers: you'll find home-made local jams, bagels, pâtés, vegetables, cupcakes and more at the outdoor stalls. Visit www.jiashanmarket.com to find out the latest schedule.

# HONGKOU JEWISH GHETTO & LU XUN PARK

*Hongkou is a thoroughly local area, almost untouched by tourism and only recently rediscovering its heritage as the locale of China's 20th-century literary uprising and as a safe haven for Jews fleeing Hitler. A fascinating walk through fast-disappearing neighbourhoods laden with history.*

**DISTANCE** 5km (3 miles)
**START** Hongkou Stadium metro station
**END** Zhoushan Road market
**POINTS TO NOTE**
Take the subway to Hongkou Stadium stop or catch a taxi to Lu Xun Park to reach the starting point. The first half of the tour is good for literary types, the second half for those interested in history. There is a real dearth of decent restaurants and cafés on this tour; convenience stores and street food are your best options while you're out and about.

**Cruise Control**

Luxury cruise ships now dock at the Shanghai Port International Terminal in Hongkou's historic dock area, which is being transformed into a high-end enclave of hotels, shops, restaurants and offices.

Just across the Suzhou Creek from the Bund, 1930s Hongkou was central enough for the International Settlement to establish its support systems here – prisons, post offices, waterworks and warehouses – but far enough away for the Japanese to establish a Jewish refugee zone and for a literary revolution to ferment.

## LU XUN MEMORIALS

Lu Xun is the father of modern Chinese literature, whose insistence on using the language of the common man in literature and railing against social injustice earned him that position. He lived in Hongkou from 1926 until his death in 1936 and is buried in **Lu Xun Park ❶** (Luxun Gongyuan; 146 Jiangwen Road; daily 6am–6pm; free), which is the centrepiece of Lu Xun territory.

Follow the signs to the tomb, where a bronze seated figure of Lu Xun welcomes visitors. His importance is signified by the inscription on his grave, by Mao Zedong. The trees on either side were planted by Zhou Enlai and the author's widow.

**Lu Xun Memorial Hall ❷** (Lu Xun Jinianguan; daily 9am–4pm; free) is a large modern hall at the eastern end of the park whose exhibitions include a replica of his study, newspaper articles and photos from the period, and translations of works by and about him.

## LITERARY LEANINGS

From Lu Xun Park, it's a short taxi ride south to the **Duolun Road Cultural Celebrities Street ❸** (Duolun Lu Wenhua Jie), a 550m (1,804ft) L-shaped pedestrian street where Lu Xun and other literary figures spent time at the teahouses and bookstores. The street is dotted with interesting structures, including Hongde Church, with its distinctive Chinese roof, built in 1928; mini-museums featuring Mao buttons, chopsticks and clocks; and a lavish Moorish-style house at the end of Duolun Road, built by Spanish architect Lafuente, which was the home of financier HH Kung.

Continue along Duolun Road to the **League of Left Wing Writers Museum ❹** (Zhongguo Zuolian Jinianguan; No. 2 Lane 201 Duolun Road; daily 9.30am–4pm; free). Founded in 1930 by a group of writers, including Lu Xun, its goal was "struggling for proletarian liberation" through writing. Located in the former Chinese Arts University where it was founded, the museum showcases the league's works and an exhibition on the lives of the martyred writers who were executed by the Kuomintang during the Communist witch hunts in 1927.

From Duolun Road, it's a short walk northeast to **Lu Xun's Former Residence ❺** (Lu Xun Guju; No. 9, Lane 132 Shanyin Road), a plain red-brick house where he lived from 1933 until his death from tuberculosis in 1936. The small, simply furnished house is in keeping with Lu Xun's character, left as it was when he lived here. A clock displays the exact time Lu Xun died: 5.25am, 19 October 1936.

### LITTLE VIENNA

Now take a taxi to **Huoshan Park** (Huoshan Gongyuan; 118 Huoshan Road; daily 6am–6pm; free) to begin an exploration of the area where some 20,000 Jewish refugees were sequestered by order of the Japanese Army during World War II. A plaque here commemorates the district as the "designated area for stateless refugees between 1937 and 1941". Just opposite on Huoshan Road, at No. 119

**Below right:**
playing chinese chess *(xiangqi)* outside a calligraphy store on Duolun Lu.

and No. 121, are the former offices of the American Jewish Joint Distribution Committee, which raised money to help relocate Jewish refugees, including the Shanghai Jews. The "Joint" still operates today (www. jdc.org).

Much of this historic district within the Hongkou Redevelopment Zone has been destroyed, but a few throwbacks remain. One block west at 57 Huoshan Road you'll find the Art Deco Broadway Theatre, where not only movies but also Yiddish plays were presented. Turn back and take a left on Zhoushan Road to soak up the bustling street life in this overcrowded neighbourhood – conditions are not

## Tilanqiao Prison

Tilanqiao Prison was constructed in 1903 by the Shanghai Municipal Government as the Ward Road Jail. With 3,000 cells, it was the largest prison in the Far East, earning the nickname "Alcatraz of the Orient". Today, it is said to be China's largest prison. Tilanqiao has six prison blocks, including one for juveniles, a hospital, workshops, an administration block, a kitchen and laundry block, and an execution chamber. First administered by and for foreigners under the Shanghai Municipal Council, it was used by the Japanese when they occupied China, Chiang Kai-shek's Nationalist government after that, and, since 1949, the People's Republic of China. Tilanqiao has been home to prisoners of war, American Navy personnel, priests, Chinese dissidents and European civilians. Despite the urban renewal all around it, Tilanqiao remains a solid presence in the area, which suggests that it will remain Shanghai's main lock-up for some time to come.

and two exhibition halls document the story. There's also a digital database of former Jewish residents for those tracing their roots.

## TILANQIAO PRISON AND XIAHAI TEMPLE

Continuing east along Changyang Road, it's just a few steps to the entrance of **Tilanqiao Prison**, on the north side of the street, first built in 1903 by the Shanghai Municipal Government and still in use today *(see box, below left)*. Do not, under any circumstances, take photos – the guards will at the very least stop you, and possibly detain you.

On the south side of Changyang Road, directly opposite the prison at No. 138, is the former Ward Road

too different from when the Jews were crammed in with the Chinese residents so that the Japanese could keep an eye on them. This was the area dubbed "Little Vienna", where European refugees established meagre cafés, delicatessens and grocery stores during the war.

A left on Changyang Road brings you to the former Ohel Moishe Synagogue, now the **Shanghai Jewish Refugees Museum** ❻ (Youtairen Zai Shanghai Jinianguan; 62 Changyang Road; daily 9am–5pm; charge). Founded in 1927 by mostly Russian Ashkenazi Jews, the former synagogue was renovated in 2007. The museum tells the story of the Jewish people who fled Europe to escape Nazi persecution and ended up in Shanghai. On the second floor, former residents share their Shanghai stories on video,

**Above from left:**
Waibaidu Bridge with views of Pudong; Astor house facade.

Heim, a shelter set up for Jewish refugees after 1939. It's now an apartment complex, but it's possible to go in and imagine the conditions of the 2,500 refugees who lived here by 1939.

From Zhoushan Road one block north, turn left (west) on Kunming Road. About halfway down the block you'll find the vibrant yellow walls and Chinese roof of **Xiahai Temple** ❼ (Xiahai Si; 73 Kunming Road; daily 7am–4pm, charge). Xiahai ("beneath the sea") is dedicated to the sea goddess, and was traditionally where fishermen would come to pray for safe returns and good catches. Enter to see the beautiful wooden carving and statuary and experience this very local temple.

Exit the temple on Kunming Road, turn right on to Tangshan Road and at the intersection with Zhoushan Road, go north on Zhoushan until you reach the lively street market. This is one of the city's last surviving street markets, with mountains of fruit, vegetables, live poultry, fish and street food – a real adventure. It's crowded, so watch your belongings and keep travel companions close.

From here, retrace your steps to Huoshan Road, from where it's a short walk to the Ocean Hotel, see ⑪① and ⑪②.

**Below:** dim sum.

## Food and Drink 🍴

**① REVOLVING 28**
Ocean Hotel, 1171 Dong Da Ming Road, 27/F; tel: 6545 8888; daily 11am–11pm; $$
Shanghai's first revolving restaurant is perfectly poised over the old Jewish ghetto for a great view. The Chinese menu includes specialities such as bird's nest and abalone, as well as a range of Shanghainese dishes and dim sum.

**② GREENERY CAFÉ**
Ocean Hotel, 1171 Dong Da Ming Road, 1/F; tel: 6545 8888; daily 6am–midnight; $$
This café offers contemporary-style cuisine with an innovative combination of Mediterranean, Continental and Asian treats. Also serves a decent buffet breakfast.

# SUZHOU CREEK

*The unassuming area along Suzhou Creek is a world away from brash, flash Shanghai. The city has evolved more slowly here, with less redevelopment, and a walk here makes a refreshing change.*

Cross over Suzhou Creek the old-fashioned way, via **Waibaidu Bridge** ❶ (Waibaidu Qiao, on the northern end of the Bund). Until 1856, the only way to cross Suzhou Creek was by ferry, but when the foreign residents of the International Settlement found that inconvenient, a British entrepreneur decided to build a wooden bridge, naming it Wills Bridge after himself. Chinese residents resented being charged a toll to cross Wills Bridge, while foreigners crossed free of charge. After the Shanghai Municipal Council bought out Wills in the 1870s and eliminated the toll, the Chineses began calling it the Waibaidu Bridge – the "free bridge". The structure we see today is its 1907 replacement, called the "Garden Bridge" by foreign residents. From 1937 to 1941, it served as the demarcation line between Japanese-occupied Hongkou and Zhabei and the rest of the International Settlement; it was guarded by turbaned Sikh policemen of the Shanghai Municipal Police on the Bund side and Japanese soldiers on the occupied side. Today, Waibaidu Bridge provides great views of Pudong to the east and Hongkou to the west.

**DISTANCE** 4km (2.5 miles)
**TIME** A full day
**START** Waibaidu Bridge
**END** Jade Buddha Temple
**POINTS TO NOTE**
Take the subway to Nanjing Road station (line 10) from where it's roughly a 15-minute walk to Waibaidu Bridge at the northern end of the Bund. Alternatively, you can take a taxi and ask to be dropped off directly at Waibaidu Bridge.

### Fare Reward

According to local lore, an Astor House bellboy, rewarded for recovering a Russian guest's wallet with a third of its contents, spent a portion of the money on a car. That car became Shanghai's first taxi and spawned the Johnson fleet, today's Qiang Sheng taxi.

## HISTORIC HOTELS

**Above:** Buddha and festival at the Jade Buddha Temple.

**Below:** Astor House

Cross the bridge on the western side to arrive at the Edwardian **Astor House Hotel ❷** (Pujiang Fandian; 15 Huangpu Road; tel: 6324 6388; www.pujianghotel.com). A modest three-star today, it was once one of the city's most elegant hotels. Spanish architect Abelardo Lafuente renovated the former ballroom, with its vaulted ceiling and stately columns, and it now makes a grand setting for breakfast. The front part of the hotel dates from 1910, but earlier buildings were the sites of numerous Shanghai firsts: the first electric light,

telephone, "talking pictures" – even Shanghai's very first taxi service. Photographs of luminaries who once stayed here line the lobby, including the likes of Charlie Chaplin and Albert Einstein.

Head across the road to the 22-storey Art Deco **Broadway Mansions ❸** (Shanghai Dasha; 20 Suzhou Road North; tel: 6324 6260; www. broadwaymansions.com), one of Asia's first high-rises. Built as an apartment block in 1934 and now a hotel, it was the location of the wartime Foreign Correspondents Club, and from its offices on the top six floors members wrote about some of Shanghai's most

### Food and Drink 🍴

**① CHAI BITES**
1/F, Embankment House, 410C Suzhou Road North; tel: 3366 3212; www.chailiving.com; Mon–Fri & Sun 10am–6.30pm, Sat 10am–10pm; $
Enjoy Spanish tapas and cocktails in the handsome surroundings of Embankment House.

**② BANDU MUSIC CAFÉ**
1/F, Building 11, 50 Moganshan Road; tel: 6276 8267; www. bandumusic.com; Mon–Fri & Sun 10am–6.30pm, Sat 10am–10pm; $
A bohemian little café serving up a simple but eclectic menu of Chinese and Western dishes, from noodles to pizza, and good coffee. It's located next door to the Bandu Music Shop.

memorable events, including watching Marshal Chen Yi and his soldiers march in to liberate Shanghai. Head up to the 18th-floor terrace for beautiful views of Suzhou Creek, the Bund and Pudong.

## SHANGHAI POSTAL MUSEUM

Head west about a block to the **Shanghai Postal Museum** ❹ (Shanghai Youzheng Bowuguan; 250 Suzhou Road North; tel: 6362 9898; Wed, Thur, Sat, Sun 9am–5pm; free; *see Behind the Bund, page 33*), the old International Settlement General Post Office and still Shanghai's main post office. The landscaped rooftop terrace affords a bird's-eye view of Suzhou Creek, Pudong, the area behind the Bund and the spreading wings of **Embankment House** *(see Behind the Bund, page 34)* a block west. Its 194 apartments once made it Shanghai's largest apartment block, and today several have been wonderfully restored and are available for short stays. If you're feeling hungry, head downstairs to **Chai Bites**, see ⑪①.

## INTO THE M50 ART DISTRICT

Exit the museum and head north on Sichuan Road. Take in the splendid Art Deco facade of the 1934 **New Asia Hotel** (entrance at 422 Tiantong Road), en route to **Bridge House** on the next block. This unassuming apartment building was the headquarters for the Kempetai (Japanese secret police) from 1941 to 1945, and included a notorious torture chamber.

Now hail a taxi and head west to the art galleries of the **M50 Art District** ❺ (50 Moganshan Road; galleries open daily 10am–6pm). The warehouses in this seedy neighbourhood on the banks of Suzhou Creek once formed the backbone of Shanghai's industry and are now the heart of Shanghai's thriving art scene. Well-known galleries such as ShanghART (Building 16; tel: 6359 3923; www.shanghart-gallery.com; daily 10am–7pm), which represents some of China's most sought-after artists, stand side-by-side with small boutique galleries offering an electic range of work. **Bandu Music Café**, see ⑪②, is located close to the

Above from far left: the Eastlink Gallery on Moganshan Road; lighting incense at the Jade Buddha Temple.

**Getting Around**
Most taxi drivers in Shanghai speak no English (unless they have a "five-star" rating, *see p.10 margin*). So it's a good idea to carry the names of all the places you want to go to in English, pinyin and Chinese characters (the Chinese characters for the driver, the English for you, and the pinyin so you can confirm what the driver's saying). Your hotel concierge should be able to help.

## Contemporary Chinese Art

China's art scene is booming, and there's no better way to experience it than with a visit to the M50 Art District. All of Shanghai's key galleries are here, covering everything from well-known artists to unknowns, photography to installation. A stroll through the area provides a free tour of Chinese contemporary art that's better curated and more current than at any museum. With each gallery eager to educate visitors about their offerings, it's a wonderful place for aspiring art students.

**Above from left:**
a large statue stands
outside the entrance
of the Art Scene
gallery in the
Moganshan Road
artist district;
Shanghai Library
Bibliotheca.

**Below:** a woman
prays at the Jade
Buddha Temple.

entrance/exit on Moganshan Road,
and has the distinction of being the
only eatery in the area.

## JADE BUDDHA TEMPLE

It's a short taxi ride south of Suzhou
Creek to one of Shanghai's major religious centres, **Jade Buddha Temple** ❻
(Yu Fo Si; 170 Anyuan Road; tel: 6266
3668; www.yufotemple.com; daily
8am–4.30pm; charge), whose brightly
hued yellow temple walls stand out

in an otherwise drab neighbourhood.
The Song-style architecture belies the
fact that this is a relatively new structure, dating from 1918.

Both the temple's popularity and its
name derive from its pair of exquisite
jade Buddhas from Burma.

Enter the walled compound through
the *san men* ("three gate") entrance.
The five halls within include the Hall
of Heavenly Kings, which has an enormous gilded image of the laughing
Maitreya Buddha, and the Grand
Hall, with the image of Sakyamuni
Buddha meditating on a lotus, flanked
by the 20 heavenly kings.

The temple's main draw is the pair
of legendary jade Buddhas, which
are housed in two separate halls.
On the second floor of the Jade
Buddha Hall is the sacred Sakyamuni Buddha, which measures a
vast 1.92m (6.5ft) and rests in a glass
case. The creamy white, almost lumi-
nous statue of the beatifically smiling
jade Buddha, draped with a gem-
encrusted robe and seated in the
lotus position, shows Buddha at the
moment of enlightenment.

On the ground floor of the Hall of
the Reclining Buddha is the other
smaller, but much more exquisite
reclining jade Buddha (96cm/37in),
depicting a tranquil Sakyamuni with
the same beatific smile at the moment
of death. The larger reclining Buddha
opposite is a polished stone version
of the original.

# XUJIAHUI

*Sitting at the confluence of eight roads, Xujiahui is an improbable mix of brash, buzzing commerce and some of Shanghai's most revered sites. Stroll through the centuries, from Buddhist temples to electronics malls.*

Meaning "Xu family village", Xujiahui is named after China's first Catholic family: Ming court official Xu Guangqi (also known as Paul Xu) was born here in 1562, and became Matteo Ricci's first noble convert and academic collaborator. Like his friend Ricci, Xu was a gifted mathematician, astronomer and linguist.

## SHANGHAI LIBRARY

The lovely **Shanghai Library Bibliotheca Zi-ka-wei ❶** (Shanghai Tushuguan Xujiahui Cangshu Lou; 80 Caoxi Road; tel: 6487 4095 ext. 208; Mon–Sat 9am–5pm; library tours Sat, but call ahead to reserve) is part of the Jesuit compound that once dominated this area. Built in 1847 on land that had been donated by Paul Xu centuries before, this was Shanghai's first public library. The ground floor of the two-storey building is designed in the style of a classical Qing-era library, while the beautiful upper storey is a fine copy of the Vatican Library. The Bibliotheca holds 80,000 volumes in several languages and includes collections inherited after their owners had fled Shanghai, including that of the

> **DISTANCE** 2km (1.2 miles) plus taxis
> **TIME** A full day
> **START** Xujiahui metro station
> **END** Longhua Martyrs' Cemetery
> **POINTS TO NOTE**
> Take the subway to Xujiahui station and follow the exit signs to the Bibliotheca. To see the old Jesuit library, go on a Saturday and call ahead to reserve a tour.

Royal Asiatic Society. There's a very fine wooden carving of St Ignatius of Loyola on his deathbed and another of St Francis in the public reading room on the second floor.

Right next door are the soaring twin towers and flying buttresses of the French Gothic **Xujiahui Cathedral ❷** (Xujiahui Tianzhutang; 158 Puxi Road; tel: 6438 4832; Sat–Sun 1–4pm; Mass (in Chinese) weekdays 7am, Sat 7am & 6pm, Sun 6am, 7.30am, 10am & 6pm). Originally called the Cathedral of St Ignatius, after the founder of the Society of Jesus order, the church has remained essentially unchanged since 1910, with the notable exception of the dramatic amputation of its 50m (165ft) twin spires and the destruction of all of its stained-glass windows during the Cultural Revolution.

The spires have been reconstructed, and new stained-glass windows created by a glass studio operated by nuns have been installed. The new panels feature Chinese images rendered as traditional papercuts, including a large rose window featuring a phoenix surrounded by the Chinese zodiac. Look high on the cathedral's exterior to see some charming gargoyles peering down.

**A Sign of the Times**
The Longhua Pagoda served as a flak tower with anti-aircraft guns during World War II, was papered over with propaganda during the Cultural Revolution, and today is surrounded by a shopping plaza.

## Food and Drink

### ① OLD STATION RESTAURANT

201 Caoxi Road North; tel: 6427 2233; daily 11am–11pm; $$$
Fine Shanghainese cuisine is served up with a slice of nostalgia in this beautiful former convent. Diners can choose to be seated in the old-world dining room or in one of two restored train cars: an 1899 German model once used by the Empress Dowager or the 1919 Russian beauty that Soong Ching Ling rode around in.

### ② BISTROW BY WAGAS

151–153A Grand Gateway, 1 Hongqiao Road; tel: 6448 2852; daily 7.30am–1am; $
Upscale bistro treats such as grilled salmon and the famous Bistrow Burger, plus delicious desserts such as carrot cake and lemon meringue pie.

### TUSHANGUAN MUSEUM

Walk south along busy Caoxi Road for a long block, passing the statue of Paul Xu, then head west (right) on Nandan Road to **Guangqi Park** (Guangqi Gongyuan; 6am–6pm). Xu was buried here in 1641; a traditional Chinese "spirit way" (row of ornamental columns and sculptures) was added to the tomb in 1903.

Continue west to **Tushanguan Museum ❸** (Tushanguan Bowuguan; 55 Puihuitang Road; tel: 5424 9688; Tue–Sun 9am–6pm; free). Located in part of the old Jesuit orphanage that taught Western art and culture to its charges – and is considered the cradle of Western art in China – this excellent museum showcases the exquisite work created at the orphanage: paintings, photographs, prints and woodcarvings. The highlight is a *pailou*, or ceremonial gate, made for the Pan-Pacific Exhibition in San Francisco in 1915 and returned to Shanghai in 2010 for the World Expo.

### LONGHUA PAGODA AND TEMPLE

Retrace your steps and cross Caoxi Road to the east side, to the former Zi-ka-wei Convent. After a tasteful restoration, it's now occupied by the **Old Station Restaurant**, see ⑪①, an excellent lunch stop. Continue north along Caoxi Road to the massive intersection, where the skyscrapers, traffic, video screens and giant adverts resemble New York's Times Square. The Grand Gateway mall here is home to deli chain Wagas's upscale **Bistrow**, see ⑪②.

Either walk or take a taxi southeast past Shanghai Grand Stage and the Shanghai Stadium to **Longhua Pagoda and Temple** ④ (Longhua Ta he Si; 2853 Longhua Road; tel: 6456 6085; daily 7am–4.30pm; charge). The dark red wood-and-brick octagonal Longhua Pagoda looks as if it popped straight out of ancient China – which

it did, since its current shape dates from an AD 922 reconstruction.

Next door stands the rambling Longhua Temple complex, Shanghai's largest and most active. Originally founded in AD 345, the Chan (Zen) Buddhist temple has been rebuilt several times and is a particularly fine example of Southern Song architecture. The current structure dates back to the 10th century.

Longhua contains some significant Buddha images: Sakyamuni Buddha's Bodhisattva form in the Hall of Heavenly Kings, and the Maitreya

Above from far left:
Golden Buddha statues at Longhua Temple; Monkey king performance at the temple.

**Botanical Gardens**
If you wish to extend your sightseeing, take a taxi 2km (1.2 miles) south from Longhua Martyrs' Cemetery to the Shanghai Botanical Gardens (Shanghai Zhiwuyuan; 1100 Longwu Road; tel: 5436 3369; daily 8am–5pm winter, 7am–6pm summer; charge). This is a rambling expanse of lakes, pine trees and more than 9,000 plants. It's noted for its bonsai collection in the Penjing Garden, the Orchid Garden, medicinal plants and a pair of 18th-century pomegranate trees. There's a memorial temple to Huang Dapo on the grounds: she was the legendary figure who brought the technique of dyeing *nankeen* cloth to the region.

**Above from left:**
Shanghai Botanical
Gardens; Century
Boulevard and Park,
Pudong.

**Below:** the exterior
of Xujiahui Cathedral,
formerly known as the
St Ignatius.

(or Future) Buddha incarnation, also known as the "cloth bag monk", in the Maitreya Hall. The temple's Grand Hall features a gilded meditating Sakyamuni Buddha set under a spiralling dome, with a statue of Guanyin (the goddess of mercy) in the rear, while the Three Saints Hall showcases the three incarnations of the Buddha.

Striking Longhua's bronze bell, cast in 1894 and weighing 6,500kg (14,330lbs), exactly 108 times to erase the 108 worries of Buddhist thought has become a Shanghai New Year's Eve tradition. The Chinese New Year temple fair has also been resurrected

here, with food, folk traditions and entertainment aplenty.

**Longhua Fashion and Gifts Market**, just north of the cemetery on Longhua Road, offers some 600 stalls over three floors selling clothing, shoes, hats, cases and much more (and yes, almost every branded item here is a knock-off, so bargain fiercely).

## MARTYRS' CEMETERY

Exit the temple the way you came in and turn right on to Longhua Road to get to the **Shanghai Longhua Martyrs' Cemetery** ❺ (Longhua Lieshi Lingyuan; 180 Longhua Road; tel: 6468 5995; daily 9am–3.30pm; free). The cemetery commemorates the "White Terror", the tragic massacre of young Communists by the ruling Kuomintang on 12 April 1927. In the early hours of the morning, they were roused from their beds and taken to the execution grounds at what was then the Longhua Garrison.

The cemetery today is a beautifully landscaped monument to the martyrs, with a blue-glass Louvre-esque pyramid and Memorial Hall. An eternal flame burns in front of a Herculean sculpture being swallowed by the earth, and the marble graves of the martyrs, many with heartbreakingly young photographs, lies in a semicircle. Exhibition rooms feature re-creations of the prison and photographs of those martyred.

# PUDONG

*Pudong is the face of 21st-century Shanghai, a showcase of the best, the brightest and the most advanced the city has to offer. A walk among the skyscrapers offers a peek into the China of tomorrow.*

Pudong is Future Shanghai. Anchored by the rocket-like Oriental Pearl Tower, this zone east of the Huangpu River with its forest of skyscrapers (not one was built before 1990) looks like the set of a space-age film. Much of Shanghai's fast-forward progress since 1990 has been telescoped into this 350 sq km (135 sq mile) area.

## SHANGHAI'S ICON

Begin your tour of 21st-century Shanghai with its iconic leitmotif, the **Oriental Pearl Tower ❶** (Dongfang Mingzhu Guangbo Dianshi Ta; 2 Lujiazui Road; tel: 5879 1888; daily 8am–9.30pm; charge). The 468m (1,535ft) television tower – China's tallest building from 1994 to 2007, when it was usurped by the neighbouring World Financial Centre – has a series of silver- and cranberry-coloured "pearls" along its length, three of which are open to visitors. Buy the RMB 85 ticket and zip up to the observation deck on the second accessible bauble, at 263m (862ft). The 360-degree view of the city is an excellent way to orient yourself, provided it's a clear day. A mediocre

**DISTANCE** 2.5km (1.5 miles), plus taxis
**TIME** A full day
**START** Oriental Pearl Tower, Lujiazui Road
**END** Shanghai World Financial Centre, Century Boulevard
**POINTS TO NOTE**
Take the metro to Lujiazui station, the Bund Tourist Tunnel or a taxi to the Pearl Tower. This is a great route for families.

revolving restaurant serving Chinese cuisine is at 267m (876ft) and above that is the third sphere (aka the "Space Capsule") at 350m (1,092ft), but it's almost too high for good views.

Your ticket also allows you entry into the **Shanghai Municipal History Museum** (Shanghai Shi Lishi Bowuguan; basement of the Oriental Pearl Tower; tel: 5879 3003; daily 9am–9pm; charge). The two-storey museum takes you through Shanghai's history, with a Chinese perspective on the imperial invaders. The museum's excellent audiovisual exhibits and dioramas include re-creations of an early stock exhange, traders and artisans at work, 19th-century cobbled streets and an arrogant tai-pan's office. There is also one of the original bronze lions from the Hongkong and Shanghai Bank and a gun from the Opium War's Wusong battles.

### FAMILY-FRIENDLY SIGHTS

If you have kids with you, head west from the Pearl Tower on Fenghe Road to the **Shanghai Natural Wild Insect Kingdom** (Shanghai Daziran Yesheng Kunchong Guan; 1 Fenghe Road; tel: 5840 6950; daily 9am–5pm; charge). Scorpions and spiders are among the creepy-crawlies, and on weekends there are interactive insect shows.

From here, it's only a few steps to **Riverside Avenue** (Binjiang Dadao), a 2.5km (1.5-mile) walkway that offers great views of the Bund. Linger at the **Kitchen Salvatore Cuomo**, see ⑪①, for gourmet pizza.

Stroll eastwards along the promenade to the **Shanghai Ocean Aquarium** ❷ (Shanghai Haiyang Shuizuguan; 158 Yin Cheng Road North; tel: 5877 9988; www.sh-soa.com; daily 9am–6pm; charge), an impressive

**Tunnel Vision**

The most enjoyable way to travel between the Bund and Pudong is via the Bund Sightseeing Tunnel: train cars are accompanied by flashing lights, waving "people" on the tracks and scenes projected onto the tunnel walls. Entrance is near the Chen Yi statue on the Bund.

facility with a focus on Chinese sea creatures, including the endangered Yangzi alligator. The 155m (509ft) marine tunnel, with sharp-toothed sharks and giant rays swimming lazily overhead, never ceases to amaze.

## JINMAO TOWER

Exit the aquarium and head southwest on Yin Cheng Road, then southwards down Century Avenue. Head past **Super Brand Mall** (Zhen Da Guangchang) at 168 Lujiazui Road, filled with a lively mix of mid-range bars, restaurants, shops and cinemas (if you have kids in tow, you might want to stop at **Element Fresh**, see ①②, for a meal). Beyond the glittering **IFC** mall with its upscale brand names, enter the **Jinmao Tower** ❸ (Jin Mao Dasha; 88 Century Avenue; tel: 5047 5101; 8.30am–9.30pm; charge). More than a decade after it was completed, the Jinmao still stands out: architect Adrian Smith wanted to evoke a pagoda. The Grand Hyatt Shanghai's 56th-floor atrium affords a breathtaking view of the building's core, rising in a concentric spiral to the 88th floor.

## SCIENCE AND TECHNOLOGY MUSEUM

From here, take a short taxi ride southeast down Century Avenue to the **Shanghai Science and Technology Museum** ❹ (Shanghai Kejiguan; 2000 Century Avenue; tel: 6862 2000; www.sstm.org.cn; Tue–Sun 9am–5pm; charge). The theme of the vast museum is "man, nature, science and technology". Five interactive halls feature everything from an exploding volcano to a mock-up of a rainforest with over 300 types of plants, plus there's a children's area.

### Century Park

Exit the museum and head south, across Jinxiu Road, to neighbouring **Century Park** (Shiji Gongyuan; 1001 Jinxiu Road; tel: 3876 0588; daily 6am–6pm), for a stroll through Pudong's green lung. Grand Theatre architect Jean-Marie Charpentier designed this beautifully landscaped 140-hectare (350-acre) eco-park, which is anchored by a huge lake.

**Mini Rates**
Ticket prices for children are most often determined by height, rather than age – if they're under 1.4m (4.6ft), they'll pay the reduced rate. Some attendants simply eyeball the kids, whereas other places have height charts to measure.

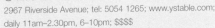

## Food and Drink

**① KITCHEN SALVATORE CUOMO**
2967 Riverside Avenue; tel: 5054 1265; www.ystable.com; daily 11am–2.30pm, 6–10pm; $$$$
Fine dining with a spectacular view: chef Salvatore Cuomo is known for his gourmet pizzas and a classic Italian menu, but what sets this restaurant apart is its setting in the shadow of the Oriental Pearl Tower. Floor-to-ceiling glass walls give every seat in the house a spectacular view.

**② ELEMENT FRESH**
Super Brand Mall, 1/F, 168 Lujiazui Road; Sun–Thur 8am–11pm, Fri–Sat 8am–midnight; tel: 5047 2060; www.elementfresh.com; $$
A relaxed setting for kid-friendly burgers, sandwiches, pasta and smoothies, plus there's a good Asian menu too.

**Above from left:**
deer diorama inside the Shanghai Science and Technology Museum; a large ball, which is actually a theatre, Shanghai Science and Technology Museum; taking in the view from the observation deck at the World Financial Centre.

## ORIENTAL ARTS CENTRE

Exit the park on Jinxiu Road and follow the signs northwest to the adjacent **Oriental Arts Centre** (Shanghai Dongfang Yishu Zhongxin; 425 Dingxiang Road; tel: 3842 4800; www.shoac.com.cn). Pudong's answer to the Grand Theatre has three theatres and an exhibition hall, and is the home of the Shanghai Symphony Orchestra. It was designed by Pudong airport designer Paul Andreu, who was inspired by nature: viewed from above, the 23,000 sq m (247,572 sq ft) building is in the shape of a magnolia, Shanghai's city flower.

## QINCI YANGDIAN TEMPLE

Hail a taxi on Yanggao Road to the **Qinci Yangdian Temple** ❺ (Qinci Yangdian Daoguan; 476 Yuanshen Road; daily 8am–4pm; charge). The traditional Chinese roof and ochre walls of Pudong's most important temple look out of place in the midst of all this modernity. The temple was first built during the Three Kingdoms period (AD 220–80) and has been rebuilt several times over the years, most recently in 2007 when the Taoist temple's Qing-era buildings were demolished and replaced with brand-new buildings and gods. The temple's most powerful deity is Yan Wang, the god of hell.

## A VIEW FROM ABOVE

From here, head back to Century Avenue to the **Shanghai World Financial Centre** (Shanghai Huanqiu Jinrong Zhongxin; 100 Century Avenue; tel: 3867 2008; observatory daily 8am–11pm, last ticket 10pm; charge), currently the world's third-tallest building at 492m (1,614ft). Enter on the western side and go to Basement 1 to purchase tickets to the observatory. SWFC's distinctive design features a trapezoidal opening at the apex, which has given the building its local nickname, "the bottle opener". There are sightseeing platforms on the 94th, 97th and 100th floors, with the latter's transparent floor offering the surreal experience of walking above the Pearl Tower. Finish up with dinner at one of the Park Hyatt's 91st-floor restaurants, see ⑪③.

## Food and Drink

**③ PARK HYATT**
100 Century Avenue; tel: 6888 1234; www.shanghai.park.hyatt.com; daily 6–10.30am, 11.30am–2.30pm, 5.30–10.30pm; $$$$
The 91st-floor restaurant, with floor-to-ceiling windows overlooking the city, has something for everyone: three menus (Western steakhouse, Chinese and Japanese), all served within the same space. The show kitchens add a real sense of razzle-dazzle to the evening.

# SHANGHAI AFTER DARK

*Experience Shanghai in all its nocturnal glory as it revels in its reputation as "the city that never sleeps" – start with a night at the theatre and end with a Bund bar crawl.*

Shanghai is well on the way to becoming a world cultural centre, with music, drama, dance and cinema all experiencing a golden age. Coupled with fantastic nightlife and a vast supply of restaurants, the options for a night on the town are almost endless.

**DISTANCE** 2km (1.2 miles)
**TIME** A full evening
**START** Grand Theatre
**END** M1NT
**POINTS TO NOTE**
Take the metro to People's Square station or catch a taxi to the Grand Theatre to begin.

## SHANGHAI GRAND

Begin your night at the dramatic **Shanghai Grand Theatre ❶** (Shanghai Dajuyuan; 300 People's Avenue; tickets: 6372 3833; www. shgtheatre.com). This modern 1,800-seat theatre features a wide variety of shows. Big names such as Tan Dun perform here, as do local drama groups, symphony orchestras, Chinese opera and dance troupes. Try to catch a performance of the Shanghai Ballet's *White-Haired Girl*.

## YIFU THEATRE

East from the Grand Theatre is the **Yifu Theatre ❷** (Yifu Wutai; 701 Fuzhou Road; tel: 6360 3195). Originally (and officially) known as the Tianchan Theatre, this is Shanghai's oldest Chinese opera house. Once

hailed as the largest theatre in the Far East, it has featured Peking opera performances since its establishment in 1925. A new 1,000-seat, two-storey theatre with modern facilities was added in 1994. Located just across from Raffles City shopping centre, the

**Above:** cocktail at the M Glamour bar.

theatre hosts troupes from around the country, but the highlight is its own Shanghai Peking opera troupe.

### Peking Opera

There are more than 360 different varieties of Chinese opera, including a popular regional version (Kunju), but Peking opera remains the best-known style. It's recognisable by its falsetto singing, vivid make-up, percussion-based music, striking acrobatics and librettos based on the exploits of legendary heroes. Peking opera was king in old Shanghai, with great stars such as Mei Lanfang, a renowned male interpreter of women's roles.

Peking opera is a highly demanding art: actors, who begin training as children, must learn not only to sing and dance, but also to acquire an extensive repertoire of highly stylised gestures and perform acrobatics. It is equally challenging to watch. Few props are used, which means the audience must use their imagination to fill in the considerable blanks.

### GREAT WORLD

Head south along Tibet Road, crossing under the Yan'an Road Elevated Freeway. On your left is the infamous **Great World Entertainment Centre** ❸ (Da Shijie), associated in the 1930s with all of the vices that earned Shanghai its moniker as the "Whore of the Orient". Built in 1918 as a

vaudeville-style multiplex with shows appealing to all ages, it was gradually taken over by the Shanghai underworld and filled with bars, opium dens and lewd floor shows.

After drugs, gambling and prostitution were virtually eliminated by the new regime in the 1950s, the Great World returned to the more wholesome fare of dramatic performances, concerts and children's shows. It has been unused for the past decade, but the municipal government has announced that the building, which was renovated before the 2010 World Expo, will be reopened. However, to date it remains closed.

### SHANGHAI SYMPHONY

Across Tibet Road from the Great World is the **Shanghai Concert Hall** ❹ (Shanghai Yinyueting). Originally the Nanking Theatre, it was one of the city's popular movie theatres during the 1930s and '40s. Today it's the venue for a wide variety of musical performances, including classical, jazz and Chinese concerts. The Shanghai Symphony Orchestra (SSO) performs its chamber music series here – try to catch a performance if you can.

### Western Classical Music

Founded in 1879, the SSO began as the International Settlement's town band, evolving into a symphony first with only foreign musicians and later with Chinese musicians. In fact, the concentration of foreign musicians in Shanghai attracted Chinese musicians from around the country and led to the establishment of the Shanghai Conservatory in 1927. It was the graduates of this conservatory that were instrumental in persuading the Communist Party that classical music could "serve the people", and continued to develop Western music in the post-1949 era.

## BUND AREA BAR CRAWL

Begin your evening at **M Glamour**, see ⓘ①, sister venue to the renowned M on the Bund restaurant. Quite possibly Shanghai's prettiest bar, Glamour's location at the top of the Bund makes it an ideal place to begin a bar crawl.

After M Glamour, turn left on Guangdong Road, walk north on the Bund to No. 18 and take the lift up to

Bar Rouge (7/F, Bund 18, Zhongshan No. 1 Road East; tel: 6339 1199; www. bar-rouge-shanghai.com; Sun–Thur 6pm–1.30am, Fri–Sat 6pm–4.30am), a favourite party spot with the jet-set crowd. The bar, decorated with lipstick-red glass chandeliers, opens out on to a spectacular terrace overlooking the Pudong skyline. DJs keep the party going until the early hours.

Leave Bar Rouge and head south on the Bund. Just one block west on Fuzhou Road is the **House of Blues and Jazz** (60 Fuzhou Road; tel: 6323 2779; www.houseofbluesandjazz. com; Tue–Sun 7pm–2am, concerts 9.30pm–1am). It's his passion for jazz and blues that drives the club, which is one of Shanghai's best venues. Late evening is the time to go, when the crowd and the music creates a real buzz. The interior feels like an old Shanghai speakeasy, with plenty of wood and a selection of vintage items from the history-loving owner's collection.

Want to keep the party going? Head west on Fuzhou Road to **M1NT** (24/F, 318 Fuzhou Road; tel: 6391 2811; www.m1ntglobal.com/club-shanghai). Perhaps Shanghai's top club, the hugely hip M1NT attracts top international DJs, visiting stars and local celebs. The club's dramatic entrance features a 17m (56ft) long shark tank, with over 20 white-tipped reef sharks. With its breathtaking, 360-degree views of Shanghai's glittering skyline, you may just want to stay until dawn…

Above from far left: the bar at M Glamour at different times of the day; Peking opera at the Yifu Theatre.

## Food and Drink 🍴

**① M GLAMOUR**

No. 5 The Bund (entrance at 20 Guangdong Road); tel: 6350 9988; www.m-restaurantgroup.com; daily 5pm–late; $$$

The cocktails are creative and the excellent food comes courtesy of M on the Bund chefs at this swanky bar-restaurant with an eclectic fusion menu. The expansive space features a trio of bars with floor-to-ceiling windows, offering spectacular views of the Bund and the Pudong skyline.

# TONGLI

*The picturesque water town of Tongli, with its ancient architecture and arched bridges crisscrossing the canals, offers a glimpse of what this region looked like back in the days of the Song Dynasty.*

**DISTANCE** 8km (5 miles)
**TIME** A full day
**START** Ming Qing Jie
**END** Luoxing Islet
**POINTS TO NOTE**
Like all of the water villages around Shanghai, Tongli is quite touristy, so try to visit on a weekday and arrive early in the morning or in the late afternoon when the tour groups have left. To get there from Shanghai, hire a car for the day; Tongli itself is entirely navigable on foot. An entrance ticket (RMB 80) is required to enter the village, and includes free entry to three sites. Book an English-speaking guide in advance via the Tongli Tourist Information Centre (512 6333 1145). Most information in Tongli is in Chinese only, so a guide will give some useful insight into what you're looking at.

**Mix with the Locals**
Nanyuan Teahouse (Nanyuan Chashe; Dongkang Lu and Nankang Lu; daily 8.30am–6pm) is a restored wooden Qing-era building that serves tea and local snacks, and offers excellent canal views from its second-storey windows. Get there early for the atmosphere: locals gather first thing in the morning to sip tea and exchange gossip.

Escape from Shanghai for a day to the beguiling old water town of **Tongli**, so pretty that it's often used as a backdrop for Chinese films and

television shows. Situated on the Grand Canal and surrounded by five streams, the built-up area is made up of seven islets, connected by a series of 49 ancient arched stone bridges with typically evocative names such as "Lasting Celebration" and "Peace and Tranquillity". This was once a wealthy place, where retired officials and native sons who had made their fortune returned to build the finely crafted grand mansions and classical gardens that make Tongli such a treasure today.

## MING QING STREET

Enter Tongli (entrance ticket required, *see left*) on **Ming Qing Jie**, named for the Ming- and Qing-era wooden houses that line it. Today, the houses are filled with souvenir shops, restaurants and snack stalls. Be sure to try the local sweet lotus root *(tongli lianou)* and sweetbread called *jiu niang bing* – decent, reasonably priced versions are available at Lin's Store and Gu Xian Cun on Ming Qing Jie. You'll want to come back here for lunch at **Xiangge JiuLou**, see ⑪①, to try the local specialities.

## GENGLE HALL

Head west on Xinzhen Jie, admiring the ancient architecture and town's signature bridges as you go. Two blocks in, on an islet, is **Gengle Hall** ❶ (Gengle Tang), evidence of the wealth that once flourished here. Ming Dynasty official Zhuxiang – who was also known as Gengle – built this mansion retreat when he retired from government service. According to local lore, he was so pleased with the result that he rarely left the 54 rooms and lovely gardens, becoming something of a hermit. Today, you can walk through the three courtyards and some of the 41 remaining rooms, but the real star here is the garden: a zigzag bridge leads to a lovely pavilion, and outside the Sweet Osmanthus Hall the scent of the ancient sweet osmanthus trees still drifts by. Buildings are arranged around a pretty lotus pond,

sited so that each has its own special view of the garden: there's a library, an art studio and a dining room.

## A TRIO OF BRIDGES

Head north a block, then east at the first right turn, to a trio of bridges: **Peace Bridge** (Taiping Qiao), **Luck Bridge** (Jili Qiao) and **Lasting Celebration Bridge** (Changqing Qiao). These Ming and Qing Dynasty "ternate" (meaning arranged in threes) bridges cross at the confluence of three rivers, creating a sort of ancient elevated highway over the water. In ancient times, it was believed that crossing the three bridges would bring good fortune on milestone occasions such as weddings and birthdays. Thus brides used to be carried across the bridges in their nuptial sedan chairs on their wedding day – and today, tourists recreate

Above from far left: Tongli is attractively lit up in the evening; and peaceful in the morning.

## Food and Drink

### ① XIANGGE JIULOU

Ming Qing Jie; tel: 512 6333 6988; daily 8.30am–8pm; $
Serves up tasty local treats, much like the many other restaurants you'll find on Ming Qing Street, but the menu is in English. The dishes come from local Jiangsu cuisine, with an emphasis on seafood. Local specialities include smoked fish, braised pig's trotters, spring rolls and dried beancurd.

that same journey, dressed in Chinese wedding garb, to the accompaniment of traditional Chinese music. Look for the couplets on Luck Bridge extolling the views.

The ternate bridges link to two mansions, **Chongben Hall ❷** (Chongben Tang) and **Jiayin Hall** (Jiayin Tang) **❸**. Tongli native son Qian Youqin built Chongben Hall, a grand two-storey house, in 1912, renovating an older residence on the property. The pretty house is smaller than Tongli's other mansions, but still has four courtyards. The highlight is its more than 100 carvings featuring symbols of good fortune, such as bats, cranes and vases, and scenes from the Chinese literary classics.

Head south across Lasting Celebration Bridge to **Jiayin Hall**, with its whitewashed walls and doorways topped with little upturned eaves. Liu Bingnan moved to Tongli and built this stunning mansion in 1922, at the then unheard-of cost of 22,000 silver taels. Jiayin's main building is designed in the Ming style, and is particularly well known for its carvings of scenes from the Chinese classical novel *The Romance of the Three Kingdoms*.

## A GARDEN FOR REFLECTION

For one of the loveliest gardens anywhere, head east for about a block and a half from Jiayin Hall to the **Retreat and Reflection Garden ❹** (Tuisi Yuan), a World Heritage site. Imperial court official Ren Lansheng created the garden in 1886, naming it after a favourite saying of Chinese officials: "When in office, one should be loyal to the Emperor; when away from office, one should meditate on his faults." The 6,600-sq m (71,000-sq ft) garden is indeed a calming retreat, dotted with ponds filled with carp, ancient, shady trees, bonsais and flowering plants. The family home is in the western part of the garden, the living rooms in the centre, and a scenic garden with pavilions, walkways and rock gardens in the east.

## AN UNUSUAL MUSEUM

A short walk directly east of the Garden is the **Museum of Ancient Chinese Sex Culture ❺** (Zhongguo Gudai Xing Wenhua Bowuguan; tel: 512 6332 2973; www.chinasexmuseum. com; daily 8am–5pm; charge), which was relocated here from Shanghai in 2004 because of rising rents in the city. The museum houses the private collection of noted sexologist and Shanghai University professor Liu Danyin, who has amassed a comprehensive collection of more than 1,200 artefacts on the history of Chinese sexuality. The well-curated museum is organised by themes such as sex in literature and the arts, and sex

and evolution. There is insight into Chinese culture, with exhibits on foot binding, dowry trunks (explicit paintings of copulating couples at the bottom of these trunks were meant as an instruction manual for newly-wed daughters), lovemaking chairs, statues and sculpture. Much of the exhibition is quite graphic.

For a different perspective on Tongli, head for the Gondolier Pier, a short walk south of the museum. You can hire a gondola (RMB 70) for a relaxing ride through the canals, sometimes accompanied by a singing gondolier.

You can also visit **Luoxing Islet ❻** (Luoxing Zhou), in Tongli Lake, to the east of the town – the price is included in your ticket. A pleasant boat ride takes you over to the islet, which has a strong religious legacy that dates back to the Yuan Dynasty. There are three temples here – Buddhist, Taoist and Confucian, all of which have been rebuilt in recent years.

**Above from far left:** Tongli's picturesque waterways and quiet streets are a welcome relief after the crowds of the big city.

**Below:** the Retreat and Reflection Garden is a highlight of Tongli.

# SUZHOU

*Suzhou's intricate mosaic of canals and classical gardens is as impressive today as it was when Marco Polo first visited and dubbed this ancient city the "Venice of the East".*

---

**DISTANCE** 6km (3.7 miles), plus taxis
**TIME** A full day
**START** Pan Pacific Suzhou
**END** Suzhou Silk Museum
**POINTS TO NOTE**

The easiest and most efficient way to get to Suzhou is on the high-speed train from Shanghai, which takes just 30 minutes. The genius of Suzhou's classical gardens is that every season reveals something different. Avoid the crowds and come during winter, when the gardens take on a stark beauty.

---

**Stunning Suzhou**
Suzhou women are noted for their beauty, from the soft melody of their Suzhou dialect to their so-called porcelain skin. The latter is believed to come from washing with Suzhou's pure well water and crushed pearls – still available in pearl shops and ground on the spot.

The ancient city of Suzhou, founded in 600 BC, flourished with the completion of the Grand Canal and neighbouring Hangzhou's emergence as the imperial capital. Silk production thrived, and imperial officials laid out classical gardens – almost 200 during Suzhou's peak. The 70 remaining gardens are now a World Heritage site and form the soul of the city – each has its own distinct personality and offers a microcosm of the world, per-fectly balanced in terms of harmony, proportion and variety.

Take an early train from Shanghai and then a taxi to the **Pan Pacific Suzhou**, see ①①, for breakfast (Suzhou Wugong Zhi Taipingyang Jiudian); tuck into the impressive buffet spread overlooking classical gardens and the evocative Ruigang Pagoda *(see below)*.

## CITY SIGHTS

Head west from the Pan Pacific entrance, then south at the Dong Dajie intersection to reach the **Gusu Garden ❶** (Gusu Yuan; 1 Dong Dajie; 7.30am–5pm; charge). Stroll through the landscaped grounds and follow the signs to the **Five Gate Bridge** (Wumen Qiao), Suzhou's tallest bridge, for the age-old view of boats and barges on the canal.

Directly across the main road is the **Ruigang Pagoda** (Ruigang Ta), a seven-storey, 37m (121ft) octagonal brick-and-timber pagoda that was first built in AD 1004.

**Pan Gate** (Panmen), the only remaining stretch of Suzhou's third-century city wall, is a short walk southwest. Climb up the 300m (980ft) of original city wall for a view of the arched bridges below.

## A CLASSICAL GARDEN

Take a taxi northeast to **Master of the Nets Garden ❷** (Wangshi Yuan; tel: 512 6529 3190; daily 7.30am–5.30pm (winter), 7.30am–10pm (summer); charge, evening performances additional fee). The name refers to the ambition of its retired court official owner, who longed to be a fisherman. The intimate garden's charm comes from its delicate, scaled-down courtyards, pavilions and rockeries. Some of Suzhou's most exquisite antique furniture is here, notably in the Peony Study, which has been replicated at New York's Metropolitan Museum of Art. From mid-March to mid-November, the garden is the setting for traditional performances of opera, music and dance. If you're there on a

moonlit night, don't miss the Moon Watching Pavilion, where you can see the moon thrice over: in the sky, in the pond and in a mirror.

**Above from far left:** views of Suzhou's ancient inner city along the Grand Canal.

## NORTH TO PINGJIANG LU

From Master of the Nets, walk north along Fenghuang Jie, turn right on Ganjiang Dong Lu – passing the twin pagodas of Shuang Ta – to reach **Pingjiang Lu**, a lovely historic cobbled stretch along a willow-lined

## Food and Drink 🍴

① **PAN PACIFIC SUZHOU**
Suzhou Wugong Zhi Taipingyang Jiudian; 259 Xinshi Lu; 512 6510 3388; www.panpacific.com/suzhou; breakfast daily 6.30–10am; $$
The Pan Pacific buffet breakfast is an impressive array of Asian and Western food served in an airy coffee shop, with floor-to-ceiling windows overlooking the hotel's gorgeous classical garden.

canal. The traditional buildings lining the street now house a range of shops, cafés, hotels and restaurants.

Follow the signs to the **Pingtan Museum** (Pingtan Bowuguan; daily 8.30am–noon, 1.30–3.30pm; free), just east off Pingjiang Lu, where Suzhou's ancient oral storytelling art comes alive. Performances are accompanied by Chinese string instruments – you don't need to understand the narrative to enjoy its beauty.

Directly next door is the **Kunqu Opera Museum** (Kunqu Bowuguan; 14 Zhongzhang Jia Xiang; daily 8.30am–4.30pm; free), which chronicles the 600-year-old Chinese opera tradition from the town of Kunshan, near Suzhou. Kunqu opera is still performed here, in a Ming Dynasty building with a stunning wooden dome embellished with an intricate seashell-like pattern. Across the courtyard, a modern building serves as a second stage and houses a display of

**Above:** silken finery at the Suzhou Silk Museum.

costumes, masks, musical instruments and an exhibition on the opera's history and key characters.

Head west two blocks, crossing Lindun Lu, to Guanqian Jie, another historic street, for lunch at Suzhou's famous **Song He Lou**, see ⑪②, renowned for its local delicacies.

### HUMBLE ADMINISTRATOR'S GARDEN

After lunch, walk north on Pishi Jie then east on Xibei Jie and Dongbei Jie to reach the **Humble Administrator's Garden** ❸ (Zhuozheng Yuan; 178 Dongbei Jie; tel: 512 6751 0286: 7.30am–5pm, 7.30am–5.30pm Mar–mid-Nov; charge, ticket includes entry to the Garden Museum). The garden is Suzhou's largest, and its name comes from a Jin Dynasty poem: "Cultivating a garden is the work of a humble man." But this 4-hectare (10-acre) garden is far from a humble undertaking. Laid out by retired Ming imperial official Wang Xianchen in 1513, the three main areas are linked by pools and ponds of varying sizes. Twisting rock-lined paths burst open on to a classical landscape: an expansive lotus pond with a view of the North Temple Pagoda, the pond crossed by zigzag bridges and pavilions perched on hillsides and in hollows.

Follow the signs to the **Garden Museum**. The four exhibition halls

## Chinese Gardens

The classical Chinese garden is a complex, nuanced thing. In the pavilions, rockeries, fish pools, gnarled trees and shrubs, and delicate blossoms are expressions of Chinese poetry, philosophy and art – each garden is supposed to be a microcosm of the world. The pine trees, for instance, symbolise long life, the goldfish money, the peony blooms nobility. Rocks and ponds always feature prominently – and no wonder. After all, the Chinese word for landscape is *shanshui* – literally, mountain water.

tell the story of the classical garden in China and feature a very interesting section on garden construction. The 24 models are fascinating.

## SUZHOU MUSEUM

Exit the museum on Dongbei Jie and head west. At the end of the block is the impressive **Suzhou Museum** ❹ (Suzhou Bowuguan; 204 Dongbei Lu; tel: 512 6754 1534; Tue–Sun 9am–5pm, no admission after 4pm; charge). The design by Chinese-American architect IM Pei, whose ancestors owned Lion Grove Garden, drew on the ancient city for inspiration. The US$40 million building is a spectacular Modernist version of a traditional Suzhou house, with plenty of glass and light, plus traditional touches such as a Chinese garden and footbridge. The museum features a collection of artefacts from early Suzhou, and includes a rare pearl stupa, porcelain, funeral relics unearthed from Dongshan Island, antique maps of Suzhou and the Grand Canal, and Song Dynasty art and calligraphy.

## OTHER SIGHTS

From the museum, head west on Xibei Jie to the intersection with Renmin Lu and **North Temple Pagoda** ❺ (Beisi Ta; 652 Renmin Lu; daily 7.45am–6pm; charge). This 76m (250ft) mustard-and-red structure on the site of Wu Kingdom ruler Sun

Quan's childhood home was first built during the third century and rebuilt in the 16th century. A climb to its summit offers spectacular views of the surrounding area – and shows how fast Suzhou is changing. The 17th-century Nanmu Hall is on the grounds, with a teahouse just behind.

Cross Renmin Lu to the **Suzhou Silk Museum** ❻ (Suzhou Sichou Bowuguan; daily 9am–4.30pm; charge), which recounts the history of silk in China. Especially interesting are the rare antique silk pieces and the section on sericulture: one room has large woven pans holding wriggling silkworms (in season) feasting on mulberry leaves, while on another shelf silk cocoons sit neatly in rows. Weavers demonstrate how young girls ruined their hands in the old days by plunging them into boiling water to separate the cocoon threads into single strands.

**Above from far left:** a cannon used by Taiping Tianguo rebels, Suzhou Museum; the Humble Administrator's Garden; exhibit at the Suzhou Silk Museum.

**Take to the Water**
The area around the Suzhou Museum is a good place to arrange boat trips on the city's pretty waterways. These depart from several areas on the rectangular main canal, the broad waterway that embraces the Old Town like a moat. None of the boat trips are a bargain, but the bigger vessels are less expensive if you don't mind waiting for them to fill up.

### Food and Drink

**② SONG HE LOU (PINE AND CRANE RESTAURANT)**
72 Taijian Nong; tel 512 6727 2285; daily 8am–9pm; $$
Suzhou's most famous restaurant, where Emperor Qianlong is said to have dined, is a good place to sample Suzhou specialities such as squirrel Mandarin fish, crystal shrimp, Gusu marinated duck, braised river eel and more. The restaurant gets crowded with tourist groups at lunchtime, so come early (11am) or late (2pm).

# HANGZHOU

*Hangzhou is a classical Chinese beauty. Its centrepiece is the beautiful West Lake, and its islands and pavilions, but it's also home to ancient temples, tea-growing villages and stylish modern enclaves.*

**DISTANCE** 16–20km (10–12.5 miles), walking and taxis

**TIME** Two days

**START** Bai Causeway, West Lake

**END** Museum of Chinese Medicine

**POINTS TO NOTE**

The frequent high-speed train service from Shanghai will get you to Hangzhou in under an hour. Once here, you can get around by taxi or hire a car. If you're a fan of tea, come in April to taste the first of the new crop of Hangzhou's famous Longjing tea.

## Food and Drink

**① LOU WAI LOU**

30 Gushan Lu; tel: 571 8796 9023; www.louwailou.com.cn; daily 9am–10pm; $$

Hangzhou's most renowned restaurant may be packed with tourists, but it still features some of the most well executed local treats in the city, such as beggar's chicken and *dongpo* pork – all with a truly unbeatable view of West Lake.

**Crashing Bore**

If unusual natural phenomena interest you, then visit Hangzhou in September. During the autumn equinox in mid-September, hundreds of people gather at a bridge near Six Harmonies Pagoda on the northern bank of the Qiantang River to watch a wall of water surging as high as 6m (20ft) – it's caused by the river's famous tidal bore.

Hangzhou was built on wealth, earned by its fortuitous position as the southern terminus of the Grand Canal and by royal privilege as China's imperial capital during the Song Dynasty. It quickly became an important centre for the silk industry and, as a favourite retreat for China's emperors, it was a place where the noble arts and leisure were cherished. Cycles of destruction – the Taiping Rebellion, which razed the city in 1861, and the Cultural Revolution from 1966 to 1976 – have been interspersed with periods of prosperity, and today Hangzhou is on the up again.

### WEST LAKE SIGHTS

Boat tours are an ideal way to see Hangzhou's legendary **West Lake** (Xi Hu) and its attractions. Row yourself or hop aboard a junk, a relaxing way to get a perspective on the lake. The boat ride will take you past Mid-Lake Pavilion and Ruan Yuan's Mound, and you can disembark at Xiao Ying Island. Here, you'll be able to see one of the legendary views of West Lake, a trio of 17th-century stone pagodas floating on the lake called Three Pools Mirroring the Moon. Disembark and head to the northern section of the lake and the **Bai Causeway** ❶ (Bai Di), named after one of Hangzhou's poet-governors, Bai Juyi. Hangzhou's famous **Broken Bridge** (Duan Qiao) stands at the entrance, so-called because when the winter snow on the bridge melts, it appears as if it has been split in two. The bridge is a favourite tourist sight, famous as the setting for the folk tale of Lady White Snake.

Continue south on Bai Causeway to the **Autumn Moon on a Calm Lake** pavilion (Pinghu Qiuyue), much depicted in paintings and one of the traditional spots from which to view the lake. A small road to the right leads to **Crane Pavilion** (Fanghe Ting), built in 1915 in memory of the Song Dynasty poet Lin Hejing, who is said to have lived here alone with only a crane for company.

### LUNCH STOP

Just to the west of Autumn Moon on a Calm Lake pavilion, stop for lunch at **Lou Wai Lou**, see ⑪①, Hangzhou's most famous restaurant, with stupendous lake views and delicious classic Hangzhou dishes – make sure you reserve in advance.

Above from far left: causeway at sunset on Hangzhou's West Lake; the Crane Pavilion.

## GU SHAN ISLAND

Bai Di causeway connects the mainland with **Gu Shan Island** (Gushan Dao), home to the impressive **Zhejiang Provincial Museum ❷** (Zhejiang Sheng Bowuguan; 25 Gushan Lu; tel: 571 8797 1177; Tue–Sun 9am–5pm; free). Built in 1929 in the Modernist Sino-Western "Nanjing Decade" architectural style, the library is located on the lush grounds of Ming Emperor Qianlong's palace, when the capital was in Hangzhou. The seven halls hold more than 100,000 cultural relics; highlights include the renowned Celadon Hall.

A short walk west is the **Xiling Seal Engraving Society** (Xiling Yinshe; 8.30am–4.30pm; free), with fascinating exhibitions of seals through the ages displayed in pavilions dotted along the hillside. Head behind the Society buildings, up the worn path to the 11-storey unrestored **Pagoda of Avatamsaka Sutra** (Huayanjing Ta), built in 1924. The lovely pagoda and surrounding area is a delightfully quiet spot where locals come for a cup of tea. Surrounded by trees, it makes a lovely spot for a break.

Head back down to Gu Shan's southern gate, where you'll find the **Sigillography Museum** (Zhongghuo Yingxue Bowuguan; daily 8.30am–4.30pm; free). The small, very modern museum recounts the history of the Chinese seal, with displays ranging from clay shards to tiny carved seals.

## TOMBS AND TEMPLES

Exit Gu Shan on Beishan Lu, where you can enjoy a drink or lunch overlooking the lake at the **Shangri-La Hangzhou**, see ⑪②.

Nearby is the **Tomb and Temple of Yue Fei ❸** (Yuefen He Yuemiao; west of Beishan Lu; tel: 571 8798 6663; daily 7am–6pm; charge), a memorial to the 12th-century Song patriot commander who, despite his success against invaders from the north, was framed, arrested and killed with his son Yueyang on trumped-up charges. He was exonerated and given a proper burial 21 years after his death, in 1163. No longer a functioning temple, its main hall is dominated by a Yue Fei

**Below:** a teahouse on the bank of West lake.

statue with a plaque in Chinese that reads: "Recover our lost territories" (a reference to Taiwan). Eight murals tell the story of Yue Fei's life. Laid out as a Song Dynasty garden, the temple is connected to the tomb grounds. The back of the temple leads to the **Temple of the Purple Cloud** (Ziyun Dong), the oldest natural cave on the ridge. From here, it's a pleasant walk into the peaceful surroundings of Precious Stone Hill (Baoshi Shan), with views of the 10th-century Baochu Pagoda (Baochu Ta) to the east.

End your day by taking a taxi to **Xihutiandi**, a restaurant, shopping and entertainment complex set in a collection of handsomely refurbished buildings that sit on the eastern shore of West Lake. This is Hangzhou's answer to Shanghai's Xintiandi, and like Xintiandi it provides an upscale experience coupled with the charm of an authentic local setting.

### DAY TWO

Begin your second day at one of China's most famous temples: **Lingyin Temple ❹** (Lingyin Si; 1 Fayun Lane; daily 5am–6pm; charge), or "Temple of the Soul's Retreat", tucked into the hills west of West Lake. This is Hangzhou's second-biggest attraction after West Lake, so try to visit early in the day to escape the worst of the crowds. The remains of the Indian monk who built the temple in AD 326 are in the seven-storey Liugong Pagoda (Liugong Ta) at the entrance.

One of China's five famous Chan (Zen) sect Buddhist temples, Lingyin has been rebuilt several times, but remarkably it was spared during the Cultural Revolution. This makes it one of the few genuinely ancient temples left in China, and it contains some of the country's rarest relics. These include the lovely 10th-century stone pagodas in front of the Hall of the Four Heavenly Kings. Inside, an 800-year-old statue of Skanda, the Guardian of Buddhist Law and Order, protects an image of the Maitreya (Future) Buddha. Go through the temple, exit via the rear door and cross the courtyard to the Grand Hall. Here, you'll find China's largest sitting Buddha: a 20m (65ft) gilded statue of Sakyamuni Buddha.

### Food and Drink 🍴

**② SHANGRI-LA HANGZHOU, COFFEE GARDEN**
78 Beishan Lu; tel: 571 8797 7951; www.shangri-la.com; daily 6am–11pm, last orders 10.30pm; $$
If the weather's good, grab a spot outside on the terrace overlooking the grounds and West Lake. There's something for everyone on the Coffee Garden's menu – pan-Asian, Hangzhou specials, Western and barbecue, all done to a high standard. Great service too.

**Boom Town**
Hangzhou is one of China's thriving second-tier cities, made wealthy by the arrival of pharmaceutical and IT companies. The result is a boom in construction, luxury hotels and malls in Hangzhou City, where you can find everything from Valentino to Tag Heuer at the Hubin International Boutique Compound.

This 1956 replica of a Tang Dynasty statue is carved from 24 blocks of gilded camphor wood.

## FEILAI FENG

From the temple, follow the signs directly south to the evocatively named **Peak That Flew from Afar** ❺ (Feilai Feng), so named because founding Indian monk Huili exclaimed that it looked so much like one in India that it must have flown here. It's easy to see his point: Feilai Feng is smaller than the neighbouring sandstone peaks.

Its origins aside, Feilai Feng's main attraction is the stone carving on the rock face. The 240 mostly intact carvings date from the 10th century to the 14th century, with the oldest ones being the 10th-century Guanyin (Goddess of Mercy) in the Deep Dragon Cave (Longhong Dong) and the carvings in Shot of Gleam Cave (Shexu Dong). But the favourite is the famous fat, jolly Laughing Buddha.

Follow the path west and the signs to Fayun Village, past the Temple of Goodness (Yongfu Si). This village has been luxuriously refurbished as the home of the Amanfayun resort where you can have lunch at the **restaurant**, see ⑪③, followed by a traditional tea ceremony featuring Hangzhou's famous Longjing tea at the **Teahouse**, see ⑪④. Take a moment and wander through the complex of restored village houses – it's eminently luxurious,

and the meticulous restoration of the thatched roofs and stone walls against the age-old landscape of mountains and ancient trees evokes the charm of old China.

## DRAGON WELL VILLAGE

The Amanfayun staff can order a taxi to take you to your next destination: **Dragon Well Village** (Longjing

---

### Food and Drink

**③ AMANFAYUN**
22 Fayun Nong, Xihujiedao Xihufengjingmingsheng District; tel: 571 8732 9999; www.amanresorts.com; $$$$
Amanfayun's high-end Western restaurant serves a gourmet selection of international dishes that change with the season, often using local ingredients. The setting, in a refurbished village house, is spectacular: with light wood and Chinese design flourishes, it's a relaxing spot after a morning of sightseeing.

**④ TEAHOUSE**
Amanfayun, 22 Fayun Nong, Xihujiedao Xihufengjingmingsheng District; tel: 571 8732 9999; www.amanresorts.com; $$$
Amanfayun's teahouse serves tea the old-fashioned way: an old-style ceremony that reveals the complexity of the drink and the rituals surrounding it. Like the restaurant, it is set in a luxuriously refurbished village house, providing a very atmospheric experience.

Cun), beginning at the **Dragon Well** ❻ (Longjing) itself. Hangzhou's renowned tea of the same name comes from the Dragon Well spring. The two levels of springs that feed the pond create a line when the water is disturbed, instead of the usual concentric circles. The pure water is said to improve the complexion – which is why you'll see visitors splashing their faces with the cool water.

From Dragon Well, follow Longjing Lu north about 3km (2 miles), past the pretty tea terraces in the village to the **China National Tea Museum** ❼ (Zhongguo Chaye Bowuguan; Longjing Lu; tel: 571 8796 4221; Tue–Sun 8.30am–4.30pm; free), just north of the village proper. The museum does an excellent job of documenting the history and culture of tea production in its five buildings. Be sure to visit the beautifully decorated tea rooms of the different ethnic minorities, one of the highlights here.

From the museum, take a taxi southeast to the lovely **Six Harmonies Pagoda** (Liuhe Ta; daily 6am–6.30pm; charge; ask the taxi to wait for you). The pagoda, which stands near the northern bank of the Qiantang River, was built in 970 in the hope that it might control the river's mighty tidal waves (it has been unsuccessful). It was last rebuilt in 1900, but the interior dates to 1123. The Song Dynasty pagoda may not have managed to stop

the massive tides, but it is still the traditional spot from which to watch the famous tidal bore during the autumn equinox in mid-September.

Continue onwards via car to **Hefang Jie**, on the eastern side of West Lake. This shopping street has recreated a Qing Dynasty setting; shops sell traditional local snacks, plus Chinese knick-knacks and souvenirs.

Just off Hefang Jie is the gorgeous **Museum of Chinese Medicine** (Hu Qingyu Tang; daily 8.30am–5pm; charge), a Qing-era building that is a working pharmacy and clinic, reputedly the oldest in China. Despite the name, there isn't much to the museum aside from a few signs (in Chinese), but go in to see the period architecture, pretty courtyards, ornate carving – and the doctors going about their business as they have done for a century.

# DIRECTORY

A user-friendly alphabetical listing of practical information, plus hand-picked hotels and restaurants, clearly organised by area, to suit all budgets and tastes, and nightlife venues. There's also a handy list of the major sights in Chinese characters.

# A

## ADDRESSES

Buildings are usually sequentially numbered, odd numbers on one side of the street and even numbers on the other. As the major streets often run the entire length of the city, it helps to know what the nearest cross-street is when trying to locate an address, such as Central Huaihai Road near *(kaojing)* Gao'an Road. It's easier with newer buildings, as the street address now indicates building numbers within an area – for example, Central Huaihai Road 1000–2000.

## AGE RESTRICTIONS

It is illegal to sell alcohol and tobacco to those under 18 years of age in China, although the law is not strictly enforced. It is not uncommon for children to be given small amounts of beer or wine at family dinners, and it is relatively easy for teenagers to buy alcohol and cigarettes without ID in shops and clubs.

# B

## BUDGETING

Shanghai is China's most expensive city, although you can still enjoy some good bargains. Accommodation can cost from as little as RMB 100 for a dorm bed to upwards of RMB 2,500 for one of the city's de luxe five-star hotels.

Similarly, a meal in a simple Chinese restaurant can cost as little as RMB 50 per person, while you can easily pay RMB 500 at the one of the city's swankier Chinese or Western eateries. Local beer costs as little as RMB 25; imported beer is three times more. A glass of wine at an expensive restaurant costs RMB 60 and upwards.

The city's efficient public transport system is cheap – a bus or metro ride within the downtown area won't cost more than RMB 5. Taxi rides are also inexpensive, running about RMB 15–30 for trips within the city centre, or slightly more after 11pm, when flag fall starts at RMB 18.

Entry fees to most attractions are under RMB 20, except for prime attractions that can cost around RMB 100. In 2007, many parks and museums stopped charging admission, and provincial art galleries across the country are now following suit. Most temples charge a nominal entrance fee.

# C

## CHILDREN

The Shanghainese love children. There is not a museum, restaurant or theatre where your child will feel unwelcome. The downside is a loss of privacy: your kids will be touched, stared at, talked to and photographed – just take a positive attitude about the whole thing and you'll meet new friends and gain fresh insights.

Hotels often allow children to stay with parents in a double room at no extra charge. Extra beds are available for a small surcharge. Reliable babysitters, called *ayi* (aunty), are easily available. If you're planning to be in Shanghai for any length of time, consider a serviced apartment with kitchen and laundry facilities.

## CLIMATE

Shanghai has a northern subtropical monsoon climate with four distinct seasons. Rainfall is plentiful throughout the year, though most of it falls during the rainy season from June to September. Expect hot and muggy summers with daytime temperatures hovering in the low to mid-30s°C (90–95°F) in July and August, and chilled-to-the-bone damp winters in December and January. January is the coldest month, with daytime temperatures usually below 10°C (50°F), occasionally dipping below zero at night. Snow is rare in Shanghai, although there are sometimes late December/January flurries.

The city's most comfortable (and sunny) weather is in spring (mid-March to May) and autumn (September to early November), although even then it is hardly reliable.

## CLOTHING

Shanghai errs on the side of casual, but it is a city of unrelenting style: you'll be forgiven for not wearing a tie, but never for looking like a bumpkin. Light, breathable clothes work best in the hot, humid summer months, with a light wrap for overly air-conditioned restaurants and offices. In winter, several layers of clothing are the key to staying warm – coats, scarves, hats, the lot. Savvy travellers always carry a foldable umbrella with them to protect against sudden showers.

## CRIME AND SAFETY

Shanghai is a relatively safe city, but petty crimes such as pickpocketing do occur in crowded areas like train stations, markets and busy streets. There is very little violent crime against foreigners, but tourists should be aware of scams that generally begin with a request from the scammer to practise their English or visit a student art exhibition. Avoid unlicensed cab drivers or motorcycle taxis.

Shanghai is a safe city for women, who are able to walk alone, even at night, without being harassed – but again, you should be on your guard.

## CUSTOMS

Duty-free allowance per adult is as follows: two bottles of liquor (75cl each), 400 cigarettes, 50g of gold or silver, and perfume for personal use. On arrival, tourists have to fill out a baggage declaration form and hand it in to customs. There is no limit to the amount of foreign currency and Chinese Renminbi traveller's cheques that can be brought in; the unspent portion may be taken out. There is a long list of prohibited items, including animals, firearms, plant material and media deemed "detrimental" to China's social and political security. For up-to-date details see www.china.org.cn. Note: antiques require a government stamp in order to be exported; most reputable dealers can take care of the necessary paperwork.

## Disabled Travellers

Most of Shanghai's modern hotels, buildings and museums are wheelchair-accessible, but older buildings and the myriad over/underpasses and walkways can present challenges for disabled travellers. Newer metro stations all have lifts or wheelchair ramps, though you may need to contact staff first to have these activated. Bashi Taxi (tel: 6431 2788) has several minivans that cater for the wheelchair-bound.

## E

## ELECTRICITY

Local electricity is 220 volts; 50 cycles AC. Chinese-to-foreign conversion accessories – whether conversion plugs or voltage converters – are easily available at department stores and hotels.

## EMBASSIES AND CONSULATES

**Australia:** 22/F, Citic Square, 1168 Nanjing Road West; tel: 2215 5200; www.china.embassy.gov.au
**Canada:** 8/F, Eco City Building, 1788 Nanjing Road West; tel: 3279 2800; www.shanghai.gc.ca

**New Zealand:** Rm 1605–1607A, The Centre, 989 Changle Road; tel: 5407 5858
**Singapore:** 89 Wanshan Road; tel: 6278 5566
**United Kingdom:** Suite 301, Shanghai Centre, 1376 Nanjing Road West; tel: 3279 2000; www.ukinchina.fco.gov.uk
**United States:** 1469 Central Huaihai Road; tel: 6433 6880

## EMERGENCIES

The police have a foreign translator on hand 24/7, so it's the best number to call in an emergency.
Ambulance: 120
Fire: 119
Police: 110

## ETIQUETTE

You could be forgiven for thinking that "anything goes" in Shanghai. But do bear in mind the following:
• Shoes should be removed when entering homes; sometimes slippers will be provided.
• Use both hands to present business cards at meetings.
• Tea should be offered when you host someone, whether at home or in a business setting.
• If you invite someone to dinner, you're usually expected to pay for the entire meal – Shanghainese only "go Dutch" with close friends or colleagues.

Fortunately, the Shanghainese are very forgiving of foreigners when it comes to local rules of etiquette, so you'll be excused most gaffes. The most serious breaches of etiquette tend to involve politics rather than manners: although the atmosphere is far more open now, it's still wise to avoid political discussions, especially involving sensitive topics like Taiwan and Tibet.

## F

## FURTHER READING

*Rise of a Hungry Nation: China Shakes the World*, James Kynge (2006). Excellent book by former *Financial Times* Beijing bureau chief explains all you ever needed to know about China's economic rise.

*New Shanghai Cuisine*, Jereme Leung (2005). The executive chef at the Whampoa Club takes a historical, and beautifully photographed, journey through the complex cuisine of Shanghai.

*Life & Death in Shanghai*, Nien Cheng (1987). Horrific autobiographical tale, written in exile, about encarceration and survival during the Cultural Revolution.

*Western Architecture in Shanghai: A Last Look*, Tess Johnston and Deke Erh (2004). Beautifully photographed book chronicling the origins and architects of Shanghai's rich portfolio of Western-influenced villas, mansions and historic houses.

*Carl Crow – A Tough Old China Hand*, Paul French (2006). Fascinating story of an intriguing character – an American journalist, ad man and social networker – who became an intrinsic feature of 1920s and '30s Shanghai.

*In Search of Old Shanghai*, Lynn Pan (1982). Historical musings about old Shanghai by probably the city's best chronicler.

*Empire of the Sun*, JG Ballard (1984). This emotive wartime story of a young boy interned by the occupying Japanese later became a major movie.

## G

## GAY/LESBIAN ISSUES

Acceptance of the gay and lesbian community in Shanghai has been tentative on an official level. Shanghai LGBT (shanghailgbt@yahoogroups. com) hosts events in the city's gay and lesbian bars.

## GREEN ISSUES

China is one of the world's worst polluters, but environmental concerns are starting to be taken seriously. On the street level in Shanghai, collecting and recycling waste materials is a means of business for many low-income senior citizens, aided by recycling bins across the city. Cycling is also a popular means of getting around the flat and compact inner city – though can be a dangerous undertaking if you're not familiar with Shanghai's crazy traffic.

China is also leading the way in solar power and other environmental building technologies. The twice-yearly grassroots **Eco Design Fair** champions sustainable producers and healthy lifestyles. Its website, www.ecodesignfair.cn, also serves as a directory and general community resource. For those conscious of their carbon footprint, Shanghai's Urbn Hotel (www.urbnhotels.com) is China's first carbon-neutral hotel – with plenty of style to boot.

# H

## HEALTH

Healthcare in Shanghai is reasonably good. There are Western-staffed clinics and designated foreigners' clinics in local hospitals with English-speaking personnel. For more serious and complicated issues, patients often return to their home countries or seek treatment in Hong Kong, so visitors to Shanghai are encouraged to have health insurance that covers repatriation expenses. You should bring all required medications during your visit, whether over-the-counter or prescription, as medicines may be sold under different names.

### Inoculations

Other than requiring a yellow fever vaccination certificate from travellers coming from tropical South America or sub-Saharan Africa, Shanghai does not require any immunisations.

The Centre for Disease Control (CDC) in Atlanta, US, recommends the following vaccines for travellers to Shanghai (see www.cdc.gov). Be sure to consult your doctor at least four to six weeks before your trip so that there is sufficient time for the shots to take effect:

**Hepatitis A** – A food- and water-borne viral infection of the liver.

**Hepatitis B** – An estimated 10 to 15% of the Chinese population carry hepatitis B, which is transmitted through bodily fluids and can lead to liver disease. The vaccine is recommended if you might be exposed to blood, have sexual contact with the local population, stay longer than six months or risk exposure through medical treatment.

**Japanese encephalitis** – This is only recommended if you plan on visiting rural areas for four weeks or more, except under special circumstances such as an outbreak of the disease.

**Rabies** – Recommended if there is risk of exposure to wild animals.

### Pharmacies and Hospitals
**Emergency/evacuation:**
**SOS International 24-Hour Service**, tel: 6295 0099.

**Emergency/general:**
**Shanghai East International Medical Centre**, 150 Jimo Road, Pudong; 24hr hotline: 5879 9999, 150 0019 0899.
**Huashan Hospital**, 15/F, Foreigners' Clinic, 12 Urümqi Road; tel: 6248 3986.
**Parkway Health**, Room Nos. 203–4, Shanghai Centre, 1376 Nanjing Road West; tel: 6445 5999.

*Pharmacies*
**Shanghai No. 1 Dispensary**, 616 Nanjing Road East; tel: 6322 4567.
**Watsons**, 789 Central Huaihai Road; tel: 6474 4775.

## HOURS AND HOLIDAYS

Offices generally open Monday to Friday 9am to 6pm. Government offices are open weekdays 9am to 5pm with a one- or two-hour lunch break. Banks may stay open until 6pm or 7pm; some currency exchange desks are open around the clock, and ATMs are everywhere.

Most large malls and department stores are generally open from 10am to 10pm, seven days a week. Smaller shops may have shorter hours. Keep in mind that most businesses are closed during Chinese New Year and other national holidays.

The list of holidays is as follows *(*denotes holidays determined by the lunar calendar)*:
New Year's Day: 1 Jan

Spring Festival: Jan/Feb*
Qing Ming: 4 or 5 Apr
Labour Day: 1 May
Dragon Boat Festival: June*
Mid-Autumn Festival: Sept/Oct*
National Day: 1 Oct

Note that the Spring Festival (or Chinese New Year) and National Day are week-long holidays. Schools and government offices are open the weekend before or after the one-week holiday. Spring Festival and National Day holidays signal a huge migration of travellers across China, and trains, airlines and hotels are booked out well in advance, so try to avoid travelling during these times.

## I

## INTERNET FACILITIES

Most hotels have either in-room WiFi or ports for high-speed internet connections. Many cafés and small restaurants offer free WiFi if you buy a coffee.

## L

## LANGUAGE

Shanghai's official language is Mandarin *(Putonghua)*. Local residents also converse in the Shanghainese dialect. English is increasingly understood by the younger generations in downtown areas (though not by taxi drivers, so

**Above from far left:** People's Liberation Army soldiers march along the riverfront promenade; watches on sale at the Dongtai Road Antiques Market, famous for old Buddhas and trinkets; the Feel Shanghai logo on Taikang Road.

always have your destinations written in characters). Street names, public transport and utilities signage is written in Chinese and Pinyin (phonetic) or English translation, as are many restaurant menus.

**Useful words:**
Hello – *ni hao*
Goodbye – *zai jian*
Please – *qing*
Thank you – *xie xie*
May I get the cheque, please – *mai dan*
Stop the car – *ting che*
I would like this one – *wo yao zhe ge*
Metro station – *di tie*
Toilet – *wei xiang jian*

## LEFT LUGGAGE

Luggage can be left at the airport and the train station.
**Pudong International Airport**: Arrivals Hall, tel: 6834 6078; Departures Hall, tel: 6834 5035.
**Hongqiao Airport**: Arrivals Hall, tel: 5114 4520.
**Shanghai Railway Station**: tel: 6354 3193.

## LOST PROPERTY

If you lose your passport, it's best to contact your consulate immediately. Some consulates have emergency 24-hour numbers for this. For items left in taxis, refer to the taxi receipt for the telephone number to call (the receipt also has the taxi number on it, which will help the company locate the vehicle).

## MEDIA

Shanghai has two daily English-language newspapers. The *Shanghai Daily* (www.shanghaidaily.com) is published locally. The *China Daily* (www.chinadaily.com.cn) is the national newspaper published in Beijing. The English edition of the Chinese-language *People's Daily* is available online at http://english.peopledaily.com.cn. Foreign newspapers and magazines are only available at the city's four- and five-star hotels and foreign-language bookstores.

Shanghai also has several free English-language publications of varying quality, most with useful listings for restaurants, bars and entertainment spots. Among the best are *Time Out* (www.timeoutshanghai.com) and *City Weekend* (www.cityweekend.com.cn). These magazines are available at many bars and restaurants around town. The online www.smartshanghai.com portal is also a useful reference.

Shanghai has two English-language TV channels. News and cultural programmes are broadcast on China Central Television (CCTV) Channel 9, while ICS is a locally produced channel with slightly more enter-

**Maps**
Free tourist maps of Shanghai in English and Chinese are available at the airport, and at the concierge desks of most hotels. The maps sold at the bookshops are usually in Chinese. Recommended is the *Insight Fleximap Shanghai*, which is laminated for durability.

taining programming, including foreign movies. Most hotels will offer a range of international cable and satellite channels.

## MONEY

The Chinese yuan (CNY) is also known as renminbi (RMB). One yuan or renminbi (colloquially called *kuai*) is divided into 10 jiao (or *mao*); one jiao is divided into 10 fen. RMB bills are issued by the Bank of China in the following denominations: one, five, 10, 20, 50 and 100. Coins come in denominations of 1 kuai, and 50 and 10 fen.

Major currencies can be changed at hotels, but you must be a registered guest, or at Bank of China and ICBC, which requires a passport. Be sure to keep the foreign exchange receipt, which is required to change your remaining renminbi back to your home currency.

International credit cards and bank cards (Cirrus, Plus, Visa, MasterCard, American Express) can be used to withdraw local currency from ATMs, which are found throughout the city. International credit cards are now accepted at major hotels and most restaurants – although many Chinese restaurants and small hotels only take cash or domestic credit cards. Cash is also king in the markets and most smaller local shops.

Locals rarely tip, and most service professionals and cab drivers don't expect tips. A service fee of 10–15% is added in hotels and some restaurants, and tipping for particularly good service is becoming more common at higher-end establishments and on private tours.

# P

## POLICE

Every neighbourhood has its own police station or post, often labelled in English. This is the place to report any crime, although you might have to wait for the Public Security Bureau officer in charge of foreigners to handle your case. Otherwise, contact the Public Security Bureau directly. See p.96 for a list of emergency numbers. Most public areas have roaming security guards that can help if needed.

## POST

Every neighbourhood in Shanghai city has a post office, recognisable by its dark-green and yellow signage. Post offices in the busiest areas, such as Sichuan Road, Central Huaihai Road, Nanjing Road and Xujiahui, are open 14 hours a day, while the Huangpu district post office is open 24 hours a day. In addition to mailing and selling stamps, post offices also deliver local courier packages. Most large hotels will post letters to international destinations for you.

**Above from far left:** the train schedule billboard in the main hall of the Southern Railway Station; police training centre.

# R

## RELIGIOUS SERVICES

Officially, the People's Republic encourages atheism. However, as elsewhere in China, there are Buddhist and Daoist temples and places of worship throughout the city, as well as mosques and Catholic and Protestant churches.

Hengshan Protestant Community Church (53 Hengshan Road) in the former French Concession and Moore Memorial Baptist Church (316 Tibet Road) at People's Square host regular multi-denominational services in English and Chinese languages. Both of these churches are beautiful, historic buildings.

Muslims gather for prayers at Fuyou Road Mosque (378 Fuyou Road) and Huxi Mosque (No. 3, Lane 1328 Changde Road).

There's also an active Shanghai Jewish Centre located in Hongqiao (Shang-Mira Garden Villa 1, 1720 Hongqiao Road).

Buddhist and Daoist temples are well frequented throughout the city and are also open to visitors – some of the most popular are: City God Temple (next to Yu Garden), Jing'An Temple (1686 Nanjing Road West), Longhua Temple in the city's west (2853 Longhua Road) and the Daoist White Cloud Temple (239 Dajing Road).

# S

## SMOKING

Smoking is popular across China, and only recently have many restaurants and public spaces brought in smoke-free policies. You can still smoke in most bars, clubs and outdoor areas, and even in some restaurants.

# T

## TELEPHONES

The country code for China is 86 and the city code for Shanghai is 21, or 021 when dialling from inside the country. To make an international direct dial call from Shanghai, dial the international access code: 00, followed by the country code, the area code and the local telephone number.

Local directory assistance: 114
International operator: 116

Most public telephones in China take prepaid phone cards, which can be used for local, long-distance and international (IDD) calls. Prepaid phone cards are available in amounts of RMB 20, 30, 50 and 100.

Most mobile phone users with a roaming facility will be able to hook up with the GSM 900 local 3G or 4G networks, with the exception of those from Japan. To avoid roaming charges, get a prepaid SIM card with a local number and fixed number of minutes. Many phone providers, hotels, convenience stores and self-serve kiosks at airports sell them in denominations of RMB 100.

## TIME ZONE

The entire country operates on Beijing time, which is eight hours ahead of Greenwich Mean Time (GMT). There is no daylight saving, so the time relative to Europe and North America is one hour less advanced in the summer months. Having a single time zone in such a large country means that on the east coast the sun rises very early.

## TOILETS

Public toilets are plentiful in Shanghai, but toilet paper often seems to be in short supply (always carry a pack of tissues with you). Payment – usually a few jiao – is sometimes required. If you're squeamish, head for a smart hotel or shopping mall, where the public facilities are almost always user-friendly.

## TOURIST INFORMATION

A tourist hotline (tel: 962020) operates daily from 10am to 9pm. Information can be patchy depending on who you get on the line. Be sure to ask for an operator who speaks English.

## TOURS AND GUIDES

Various cruises on the Huangpu River and Suzhou Creek offer views of the rapidly changing cityscape along the banks of the city's two main waterways. We recommend the Huangpu River cruises for the best views of the Bund and some jaw-dropping crane action at the world's busiest container port. These leave from the Shiliupu Wharf, conveniently situated on the South Bund.

For a city tour with a difference, Shanghai Sideways (tel: 138 1761 6975; www.shanghaisideways.com) offers tours of the city's historic neighbourhoods in vintage motorcycle sidecars. The fabulous Changjiang 750s are replicas of Russian Ural sidecars and were formerly used by the People's Liberation Army.

You can explore Shanghai's fascinating Jewish heritage on a walking tour with Israeli documentarian and photojournalist Dvir Bar-Gal, conducted in English or Hebrew (www. shanghai-jews.com)

## TRANSPORT

Shanghai has an easy-to-use and well-priced public transport system. Roads and even footpaths can be hazardous, so be careful when negotiating traffic lights and pedestrian crossings as cars seldom give way. Driving is not recommended for visitors.

**Above from far left:** the city is constantly on the move; flags at Jing An temple.

## Getting Around

**Bus:** Shanghai's bus system can be confusing for visitors, and bus routes are in Chinese characters only. Taxis, which are cheap, and the metro are better options.

**Metro:** Thanks to a pre-Expo 2010 infrastructure boom, Shanghai has the longest metro system in the world. The city currently has 11 metro lines (with several more under construction) running all across the city from around 6am to midnight. Everything is signposted in English and Chinese, and on-train stop announcements are multilingual. Metro line 2 connects Pudong International Airport in the east with Hongqiao Airport in the far west.

Purchase a ticket at the machines in each subway station (you can press a button for English and follow the prompts). Have plenty of coinage on you, as only some machines accept notes. Alternatively, you can purchase a stored-value Shanghai Transportation Card, which can also be used for taxis, buses and ferries.

**Taxis:** Taxis are easy to hail on the street outside rush hour – Dazhong (tel: 96822) and Jingjiang (tel: 96961) are reputable companies. Fares are cheap, straightforward and always metered, and receipts are given if requested. Flagfall is RMB 14 (RMB 18 after 11pm). Tipping is not expected. Keep the taxi receipt, which has each driver's licence number printed on it, in case you leave something behind in the car.

## Arriving by Air

Shanghai has two airports (www.shairport.com): Pudong International Airport (30km/19 miles east of the city – code PVG) is mainly for international flights; Hongqiao Airport (15km/9 miles west of the city – SHA) is for domestic flights and some Hong Kong, Taiwan and South Korean routes. Getting from both airports to the city is straightforward. From Pudong, official taxis into the city cost RMB 100–200, depending on your destination. The Maglev train (one way RMB 50, or RMB 40 with same-day air ticket) links with Longyang Road metro station (Line 2) in Pudong – from here, you can catch a metro or taxi to your onward destination. Ten air-conditioned airport bus routes transport passengers around the city (route details are posted in the arrivals hall). From Hongqiao, the Hongqiao Transport Hub connects Terminal 2 with metro lines 2 and 10, Hongqiao railway station and the long-distance bus station. Terminal 1 connects with metro line 10 only. Taxis are easily available and cost RMB 20–100 to downtown, depending on the final destination.

## Arriving by Sea

Set to become a major cruise destination, Shanghai has built the Shanghai

Port International Cruise Terminal on the North Bund and another terminal on Potai Bay in Wusong Port to handle the larger vessels that are unable to pass under the Yangpu Bridge. A third terminal is located at the mouth of the Yangtze.

## Arriving by Train

Train services have improved dramatically in recent years, cutting travel time by hours to nearby locations such as Suzhou, Hangzhou and Nanjing. Shanghai to Beijing bullet trains depart several times a day, with a journey time of less than five hours. Most high-speed trains use Hongqiao railway station, a sparkling new hub in the city's west that integrates with the domestic airport, metro, taxis and long-distance buses.

Tickets can be purchased at the railway stations or official ticketing counters throughout the city up to 10 days ahead of the date of travel. You'll need to present your passport at the time of purchase (your passport number will be printed on your ticket), as well as on the train. Most hotels can obtain train tickets for guests. If you change plans, tickets can be exchanged for a different time train up until a few minutes before the train departs.

## Car Hire

You need a Chinese licence to drive in China and, besides, it's not for the faint-hearted. Dangerous driving is rampant. Avis (www.avischina.com) operates throughout Asia, offering self-drive options and cars that come with experienced drivers.

## VISAS

Apply for visas in your home country prior to arriving in China. Hong Kong is a convenient alternative. A single-entry, 30-day visa is usually provided for those with passports with a minimum of six months' validity. Double-entry or multiple-entry visas are more expensive and more difficult to obtain.

## WEBSITES

The following websites provide a variety of information on travel-related subjects on Shanghai.

**General Information**
www.china.org.cn

**China Foreign Ministry**
www.fmprc.gov.cn/eng

**Shanghai Government**
www.shanghai.gov.cn
www.meet-in-shanghai.net

**Hotel Bookings**
www.ctrip.com
www.elong.net

**Weights and Measures**
The metric system is used across China. Traditional measurements, such as *jin* (approximately 500g) are sometimes used when buying food.

Shanghai has surged to the top of the global hotel scene, as most of the world's finest international chains have hurried to open brand-new flagship properties in this mega city. They are joined by Asia's top serviced apartment companies, which offer more space, and kitchens, along with some hotel-style services. Many Chinese operators have pitched in with fine properties of their own, some of them in heritage buildings, or in villa compounds with spacious grounds. Quirky boutique hotels and no-frills budget chains round out the city's offerings. Booking websites www.ctrip.com and www.elong.net offer easy booking and competitive prices.

## The Bund

### Astor House Hotel (also called Pujiang Hotel)

15 Huangpu Road; tel: 6324 6388; www.pujianghotel.com; $

One of Shanghai's oldest – and best-value – hotels. Albert Einstein, Ulysses S Grant, Bertrand Russell and Charlie Chaplin are all said to have stayed, and it was home to the first electric lights in China. The atmospheric old building

Price for a double room for one night without breakfast:

| | |
|---|---|
| $$$$ | over RMB 1200 |
| $$$ | RMB 900–1200 |
| $$ | RMB 600–900 |
| $ | below RMB 600 |

just north of the Bund is ripe for a revamp, but stay before that happens because for now this wonderful old gem is still in a reasonably authentic state and offers good value for money. Rooms differ greatly – from stark to ornate.

### Captain Hostel

37 Fuzhou Road; tel: 6323 5053; www.captainhostel.com.cn; $

A great location near the riverfront and a few minutes from Nanjing Road. Accommodation ranges from basic "Sailor Bunks" to standard rooms. Even if you don't stay, the rooftop Captain's Bar, with its Pudong views and cheap drinks, is a welcome antidote to the glitz of its flashier neighbours.

### Fairmont Peace Hotel

20 Nanjing Road East, corner Nanjing Road and the Bund; tel: 6321 6888; www.fairmont.com/peacehotel; $$$$

Shanghai's most famous hotel, dating back to 1929, has a striking Art Deco facade and iconic green copper dome. After a three-year makeover, the hotel was finally restored to its former glory in 2010. Although the rooms are small for the price tag, the place is dripping with history.

### Hotel Indigo Shanghai on the Bund

585 Zhongshan East (No. 2) Road; tel: 3302 9999; www.shanghai.hotel indigo.com; $$$$

This 30-storey, 184-room hotel is so close to the water that it feels like you're floating, and it stands out for its sweeping views and deft local design touches, plus a winning rooftop bar and steakhouse. It's on the South Bund, a short taxi hop to the Bund proper and close to the Old Town.

## Hyatt on the Bund

199 Huangpu Road; tel: 6393 1234; www.shanghai.bund.hyatt.com; $$$$
When it opened in 2007, this funky riverfront property became the first five-star hotel in the up-and-coming Hongkou district, just north of the Bund. Xindalu restaurant serves the city's best Peking duck, and the top-floor bar and many of the rooms have spectacular views of the Bund and Pudong riverbanks.

## Peninsula Shanghai

32 Zhongshan East (No. 1) Road; tel: 2327 2888; www.peninsula. com; $$$$
At the head of the Bund, the stone edifice that houses the Peninsula is half a century younger than its illustrious neighbours, but this exquisite five-star hotel has a timeless Art Deco ambience. Rooms are packed with high-tech luxuries such as internet phones and humidifier controls.

## Sofitel Hyland

505 Nanjing Road East; tel: 6351 5888; www.sofitel.com; $$

Located on Nanjing Road pedestrian street, this four-star hotel has 400 tastefully decorated rooms with comprehensive facilities.

## Waldorf Astoria Shanghai on the Bund

No. 2 The Bund, Zhongshan East No. 1 Road; tel: 6322 9988; www. waldorfastoriashanghai.com; $$$$
Housed in a neoclassical Bund building that served as a British gentlemen's club in the 1920s, this exquisite five-star opened in 2010 and features modern-day comforts in a timeless setting. Don't miss a tipple at the Long Bar, a legendary Shanghai drinking institution.

## The Waterhouse at South Bund

Nos. 1–3 Maojiayuan Road, Zhongshan Road South; tel: 6080 2988; www.waterhouseshanghai.com; $$$$
Set in a 1930s dockyard factory beside the Huangpu River on the South Bund, this 19-room designer hotel features industrial-glam interiors and an excellent Mediterranean restaurant.

## The Westin Bund Centre

88 Central Henan Road; tel: 6335 1888; www.starwood.com; $$$$
Its readily recognisable pineapple-shaped crown is visible across the city, and the hotel is equally well

**Above from far left:** a de luxe room at the Peninsula Shanghai; the Peninsula's pool terrace.

known for its landmark Sunday brunch, which features choices from every corner of the globe, spiced up with Chinese dancers, acrobats and jugglers. A comfortable and well-placed choice between the Bund and People's Square.

People's Square Area

### Citadines Shanghai Jinqiao

55 Beijing Road West; tel: 2308 6666; www.citadines.com; $

The least expensive of the three serviced apartment brands offered by Singapore-based Ascott International, but it's perfectly adequate, especially for long-stay visitors on a budget. This property has comfortable apartments ranging from studios to two-bedrooms, with modern amenities and fully equipped kitchens.

### JW Marriott

399 Nanjing Road West; tel: 5359 4969; www.marriotthotels.com/shajw; $$$$

JW Marriott Shanghai Tomorrow Square is a hotel-in-a-tower, with an elegant main lobby on the 38th floor. The rooms feature silk textured wallpaper, mahogany tea chests and marble tubs to go with the business-oriented amenities such as laptop-sized room safes and multiple telephones. Don't miss JW's Lounge on the 40th floor, which has a 50-strong Martini menu and fine views of the city.

### Langham Yangtze

740 Hankou Road; tel: 6080 0800; www.langhamhotels.com; $$$$

So this is what the gilded age looked like: located in a 1934 Art Deco building, this pocket-sized hotel has gorgeous Art Deco-inspired interiors. Some of the rooms have balconies, and all of them feature bold 1930s-style designs coupled with soft, padded luxury.

### Le Royal Méridien

789 Nanjing Road East; tel: 3318 9999; www.starwood.com; $$$$

This dramatic, ultra-modern 60-storey tower on the corner of People's Park and Nanjing Road has plush interiors filled with artwork. The bars and restaurants are shaped by the exterior angles of the building, which lend them a unique ambience.

Nanjing Road West Area

### Baolong Home Hotel

125 Nanyang Road; tel: 5174 8188; $

Tucked away behind the Portman Ritz-Carlton, this small-budget hotel is part of a well-managed local chain. Its clean, comfortable rooms and superb location belie the very reasonable rates.

### JIA Shanghai

931 Nanjing Road West; tel: 6217 9000; www.jiashanghai.com; $$$$

A quirky little hotel in a 1920s-era building, JIA Shanghai is filled with playful design details in bright primary colours. The 55 rooms are similarly eclectic, with polished black counters, green ottomans and snow-white beds with mustard-yellow duvets.

### Portman Ritz-Carlton

1376 Nanjing Road West; tel: 6279 8888; www.ritz-carlton.com; $$$$

Located in the Shanghai Centre, this recently renovated hotel combines smooth luxury with a location on Nanjing Road, surrounded by a wealth of sightseeing and dining choices.

### PuLi Hotel and Spa

1 Changde Road; tel: 3203 9999; www.thepuli.com; $$$$

Right in the heart of the Puxi CBD, near Nanjing Road and overlooking Jing'An Park, this dazzling hotel has a seductive modern oriental style.

### Shanghai Centre

1376 Nanjing Road West; tel: 6279 8600; www.shanghaicentre.com; $$–$$$$

An excellent and little-known accommodation option within the same complex as the Portman Ritz-Carlton on Nanjing Road West. A genuine bargain, the apartments offer short-term stays in a variety of rooms, from studios to three-bedroom suites.

### Urbn Hotel

183 Jiaozhou Road; tel: 5153 4600; www.urbnhotels.com; $$$$

China's first carbon-neutral hotel is far more environmentally friendly than the former factory it replaced. Design-wise, the little boutique property is an effortless success – smooth and compelling without trying too hard.

## Xintiandi & Old Town

### 88 Xintiandi

380 Huangpi Road South; tel: 5383 8833; www.88xintiandi.com; $$$$

A refreshing departure from the chain hotels, this boutique residence in the heart of Xintiandi has a charming oriental design, high-tech electronics and kitchenettes. Try to get a room with a balcony.

### Oriental Bund Hotel

386 Renmin Road; tel: 6333 8888; www.orientalbundhotel.com; $

It won't win any style awards, but this mid-level hotel is well priced, with stark but comfortable rooms, a small gym, business centre and a convenient location not far from Yu Garden.

### Shama Luxe at Xintiandi

168 Shunchang Road; tel: 2320 6688; www.shama.com; $$–$$$$

One-, two- and three-bedroom long-stay apartments in styles ranging from

**Above from far left:** PuLi Hotel and Spa; five-star spa Tea Treatment; the pool at Le Royal Méridien.

| Price for a double room for one night without breakfast: | |
| --- | --- |
| $$$$ | over RMB 1200 |
| $$$ | RMB 900–1200 |
| $$ | RMB 600–900 |
| $ | below RMB 600 |

traditional to ultra-modern pads. All rooms have fully equipped kitchens, and the property also features a gym, spa, swimming pool and other hotel-style features.

Former French Concession

### City Hotel

5–7 Shaanxi Road South; tel: 6255 1133; $

Three-star hotel with a great mid-city location, business facilities, Chinese and Western cuisine and a disco.

### Hengshan Hotel

534 Hengshan Road; tel: 6437 7050; $$

Formerly the Picardie Mansions, this Art Deco-style hotel is located on tree-lined Hengshan Road. Offers adequate rooms, Western and Chinese restaurants, a business centre and a health club.

### Hilton Shanghai

250 Huashan Road; tel: 6248 0000; www.hilton.com; $$$

A venerable hotel that has established itself as an accommodation landmark, the Hilton has a convenient location between the former French Concession and Jing'An Temple. Well managed and always buzzing, it has good restaurants, a skylit pool and penthouse bar.

### Jin Jiang Hotel

59 Maoming Road South; tel: 3218 9888; www.jinjianghotels.com; $$

The Jin Jiang's buildings were some of the former French Concession's most popular addresses. Rooms are comfortable and homely but not luxurious, with the exception of the Grosvenor House, which offers the most decadent suites at the most decadent prices. Its history trumps the rooms: Richard Nixon and Mao Zedong signed the Shanghai Communiqué here in 1972.

### Mansion Hotel

82 Xinle Road; tel: 5403 9888; www.chinamansionhotel.com; $$$$

The Mansion is a grand hotel in miniature, small in stature but large in palatial trappings and old-world charm. The 1920s-era building has just 30 rooms, but its garden courtyard, high-ceilinged lobby and dressy doormen evoke images of classic grandeur, while the rooms feature wood floors, antique mirrors and chandeliered ceilings.

### Taiyuan Villa

160 Taiyuan Road; tel: 6471 6688; www.ruijinhotelsh.com; $$

One of the nicest mansions in the

| Price for a double room for one night without breakfast: | |
| --- | --- |
| $$$$ | over RMB 1200 |
| $$$ | RMB 900–1200 |
| $$ | RMB 600–900 |
| $ | below RMB 600 |

former French Concession dating back to the 1920s, Taiyuan Villa was once the home of General George Marshall, as well as Mao's dragon-lady fourth wife, Jiang Qing (though not at the same time). Refurbished using 1930s-style Shanghai furniture, the rooms overlook the villa's sprawling lawns.

### Xijiao State Guesthouse

1921 Hongqiao Road; tel: 6219 8800; www.hotelxijiao.com; $$$

What sets this place apart is its picturesque setting in an 80-hectare (200-acre) woodland park. There are stylish rooms as well as villas, the latter for long-term guests and scattered throughout the beautiful grounds. A 20-minute drive from the city centre.

### Marriott Executive Apartments Union Square

506 Shangcheng Road, Pudong; tel: 2899 8888; www.marriot.com; $$$$

Well-equipped and stylish serviced apartments ideal for short-term stays. The price is similar to nearby high-end hotels, but guests get a separate bedroom, kitchen, living room and other apartment-style perks.

### Park Hyatt Shanghai

100 Century Avenue; tel: 6888 1234; www.parkhyattshanghai.com; $$$$

Shanghai's highest hotel, on the 79th–93rd floors of the Shanghai World Financial Centre, is an exclusive retreat above the clouds, with chic, minimalist guestrooms and excellent restaurants.

### Pudong Shangri-La

33 Fucheng Road; tel: 6882 6888; www.shangri-la.com; $$$$

A fine five-star with a superb location, the Shangri-La has spacious rooms, first-class service, good views and some of the best dining in the city, along with a superior on-site Chi Spa. Hint: try the Himalayan Bath.

### Ramada Pudong Airport

1100 Qihang Road; tel: 3849 4949; www.ramadaairportpd.com; $$

Close to the gateway Pudong Airport, this hotel is a boon for travellers with tight flight connections. There is a full range of restaurants and a health club, and all the TVs receive instant flight information.

### The Ritz-Carlton Shanghai, Pudong

8 Century Avenue, Pudong; tel: 2020 1888; www.ritzcarlton.com; $$$$

Above the Shanghai IFC on the Pudong riverfront, this five-star features a modern Art Deco design, high-tech rooms with magnificent views (book a Bund-facing room), plus a stunning alfresco rooftop bar, Flair. There's also an excellent shopping mall and a metro station in the basement.

**Above from far left:** Bund view room at the Pudong Shangri-La; roof terrace at the Swatch Art Peace Hotel.

Few cities on earth can match Shanghai for its range and variety of food. Excellent sit-down meals of meat dumplings or soup noodles, with a pot of hot tea, can be had for handful of loose change. Meanwhile at the high end, the world's top chefs have flocked to the city, where they have opened elegant flagship venues that serve some of the most refined cuisine on the planet. And in the affordable middle lies a rich treasure trove of regional Chinese cuisines and Western selections from around the globe – many of them served in surprising venues that could only be found in Shanghai.

## The Bund

### Jean Georges

4/F, Three on the Bund, 3 Zhongshan East (No. 1) Road; tel: 6321 7733; www.threeonthebund.com; $$$

This classy Bund institution by celebrity chef Jean-Georges Vongerichten is the epitome of refined elegance, a world of just-right ingredients expertly mixed and matched, and guaranteed to set the taste buds tingling with delightful flavour combinations.

### Lost Heaven on the Bund

17 Yan'an East Road; tel: 6330 0967; www.lostheaven.com.cn; $$

You may get lost in the vast, lush interiors of this "Mountain Mekong" restaurant, which serves recipes and ingredients from Yunnan province,

northern Thailand and Burma in a luxurious, three-storey setting near the Bund waterfront.

### M on the Bund

7/F, 5 Zhongshan East (No. 1) Road; tel: 6350 9988; www.m-restaurantgroup.com; $$$

This time-honoured venue has become famous for its honest Australian-inspired cuisine, featuring fresh ingredients and straightforward preparations, served in a classy Bund setting. Book an outdoor table during good weather, and be sure to try the crispy suckling pig and the pavlova.

### Mr and Mrs Bund

6/F, Bund 18, Zhongshan East (No. 1) Road; tel: 6323 9898; www.mmbund.com; $$$

Shanghai celebrity chef Paul Pairet prepares modern French food with a tiny touch of the unexpected in this Bund 18 hotspot. Behind a big red door, the whimsical interiors with riverfront views set the scene for a memorable Shanghai meal.

### Table No. 1

The Waterhouse at South Bund, 1–3 Maojiayuan Road, Zhongshan Road South; tel: 6080 2918; www.tableno-1.com; $$$

Tasty mod-Euro restaurant by London chef Jason Atherton, former frontman for Gordon Ramsay. His first solo venture occupies an industrial-chic

50-seat restaurant in boutique hotel The Waterhouse at South Bund.

### Ultraviolet

"Secret" location; book via www. uvbypp.cc; $$$

A truly unique gourmet experience. French chef Paul Pairet (of Mr and Mrs Bund fame, see above) presents a 20-course avant-garde set menu that mixes fine dining with multi-sensorial technologies for just 10 diners each night. Book online.

### Xindalu

Hyatt on the Bund, 199 Huangpu Road; tel: 6393 1234; $$$

Shanghai's finest duck comes from the date-wood ovens of this sleek hotel restaurant on the North Bund. Their Beggar's Chicken is also a classic.

## Nanjing Road West Area

### Gongdelin

445 Nanjing Road West; tel: 6327 0218; $

Gongdelin has been serving vegetarian specialities for over 50 years. The "duck" and "beef" dishes look like the real thing, but are in fact made from tofu.

Price for a two-course meal per person, with one drink:

$$$  over RMB 200
$$   RMB 100–200
$    RMB 50–100

### Gourmet Café

1376 Nanjing Road; tel: 6298 5733; www.gourmet-café.com; $$

Serves the best hamburgers in town. Choose from 30 varieties made with house-ground meats. Don't miss the creamy milkshakes too.

### Lynn

99-1 Xikang Road; tel: 6247 0101; $

Traditional and updated Shanghainese food in in a smartly styled downtown location. Book ahead for the popular unlimited weekend dim sum brunch.

### Yang's Fry Dumpling

2/F, 54–60 Wujiang Road, near Maoming Road; $

Shanghai's favourite haunt for its trademark pan-fried snack, *sheng jian mantou* dumplings.

## Old Town

### Lubolang

115 Yuyuan Road, near Mid-Lake Teahouse, Yu Garden; tel: 6328 0602/6355 7509; $$

This rambling, old-school Shanghainese restaurant has prime views of the Mid-Lake Teahouse, curt but efficient old waiters, and a menu filled with Shanghainese favourites, including lion's-head meatballs, red-cooked pork and steamed pomfret.

### Nan Xiang

85 Yuyuan Road, near Mid-Lake Teahouse, Yu Garden; tel: 6355 4206; $

Above from far left: "Chun Juan" fried dumplings; designer flair at Mr & Mrs Bund; *xiao long bao* dumplings, Nan Xiang restaurant.

## Dumpling technique

There is an art to eating Shanghai's *sheng jian mantou* dumplings (as served at Yang's Fry Dumpling restaurant, and numerous other establishments). Filled with pork and hot broth, they are shallow-fried in wide black pans. Take a small bite of the skin first to let the steam escape and carefully suck out the scalding soup before dipping in black vinegar and popping the whole dumpling in your mouth.

A packed three-storey venue with a reputation for serving the best steamed *xiao long bao* dumplings in town. There's a takeout on the first floor, a sit-down diner on the second serving basic dumplings, and more elaborate variations (eg crab roe) on the top floor.

### Xintiandi

### Crystal Jade

2/F, South Block, Lane 123 Xinye Road; tel: 6385 8752; www.crystal jade.com; $$

Crystal Jade, of which this is one of several branches, features Shanghainese and Cantonese offerings served in an upscale setting. Try the excellent dim sum treats, *dan dan mian* (spicy noodles in peanut sauce) and *jie lan* (a steamed southern vegetable).

### Soahc

Bldg 3, South Block, Lane 123 Xingye Road; tel: 6385 7777; $$

Taiwanese owner Lily Ho was once a famous Hong Kong movie star, who later resurfaced as a restaurateur with this beautifully designed venue. Specialities include an exceptional, melt-in-your mouth lion's-head meatball with crab meat, while the lotus root appetiser and the subtly spicy Sichuan smoked duck are superb.

### Xin Ji Shi

Bldg 9, North Block, Lane 123 Xingye Road; tel: 6336 4746; $$

Xin Ji Shi has multiple outlets serving classic local cuisine: rich stewed pork ribs, crab-egg tofu, lion's-head meatballs and all the rest. The Xintiandi branch is considered to be the best in the city.

### Former French Concession

### Cantina Agave

291 Fumin Road and Changle Road; tel: 6170 1310; www.cantinaagave. com; $$

A colourful cantina with a sunny pavement patio serving Mexican staples washed down with strong margaritas and 53 tequilas by the glass.

### Charmant

1418 Central Huaihai Road, near Fuxing Road; tel: 6431 8107/6431 8027; $$

Serves Taiwanese comfort food, such as oysters in black bean and scallion, taro cakes, spicy pork with young bamboo shoots, in a city-centre location. Stays open late.

### Cha's

30 Sinan Road, near Huaihai Road; tel: 6093 2062; $

Straight out of old Kowloon, this cute

Price for a two-course meal per person, with one drink:

| | |
|---|---|
| $$$ | over RMB 200 |
| $$ | RMB 100–200 |
| $ | RMB 50–100 |

1950s-styled "canting" churns out canto classics – soup noodles, roast chicken, milk tea – until 2am each day. Be prepared to queue.

## Cheng Cheng's Art Salon

164 Nanchang Road, near Sinan Road; tel: 6328 0602; $$

A cosy, art-filled salon serving equally out-of-the-box Shanghainese and Sichuan fare, free of MSG.

## Chun

124 Jinxian Road, near Maoming Road; tel: 6256 0301; $–$$

Chun is like eating in the home of a Chinese grandmother: it has four tiny tables, and you eat what the owner, Ms Qu, has bought fresh in the market that day. The offerings are sweet, heavy, oily and unapologetically Shanghainese, such as snails, eel, fish and pork ribs. There are two evening seatings, and reservations are required.

## Di Shui Dong

56 Maoming Road, near Changle Road; tel: 6253 2689; $

This fiery favourite specialises in Hunan cuisine (similar to Sichuan, but less well known), and with its rustic decor and boisterous atmosphere, really packs 'em in. The cumin-encrusted ribs are the signature dish. Reserve in advance.

## Franck

Ferguson Lane, 376 Wukang Road; tel: 6437 6465; www.franck.com.cn; $$$

French brasserie cuisine, such as beef tartare, confit de canard and roast chicken, that is beautifully executed and served in a casual-chic space complete with brusque French-speaking waiting staff.

## Guyi Hunan

87 Fumin Road, near Julu Road; tel: 6249 5628; $$

This sparkling little restaurant, with its monumentally spicy food, is a good place for a lively dinner. The dishes served up at Guyi are more refined and less oily than most of the city's spicy offerings.

## Haiku by Hatsune

28B Taojiang Road, by Hengshan Road; tel: 6445 0021; $$–$$$

Japanese treats and cutting-edge decor on one of the old Concession's most charming cobbled streets, surrounded by a wealth of after-dinner drinking options. The fusion-inspired sushi is bold and original.

## Jesse Restaurant

41 Tianping Road, near Huaihai Middle Road; tel: 6282 9260; $$

This charming hole in the wall serves some of the tastiest Shanghainese food in town – red-cooked pork ribs, stir-fried vegetables, steamed fish – as evidenced by the clusters of hungry people waiting outside. A precursor

**Above from far left:** dim sum in Xintiandi; artfully displayed homeware in an upmarket store; Uighur bread – many of China's minority groups, such as the Uighur, form part of the Shanghai community.

to the fancier Xin Ji Shi restaurants, it is small, plain and unpretentious, but it really is one of the best.

### Noodle Bull

291 Fumin Road; near Xinle Road; tel: 6170 1299; $

A great option for a quick and tasty lunch, this cool, contemporary noodle joint serves deep bowls of hand-pulled noodles and tasty sides. Wash these down with the house plum juice.

### Shintori

803 Julu Road, near Fumin Road; tel: 5404 5252; $$$

Shintori has a beautifully presented bamboo-bedecked entrance that leads to a large, open dining room with an open kitchen that turns out a fine selection of sushi and sashimi, along with updated versions of other Japanese classics.

### Sichuan Citizen

30 Donghu Road, near Huaihai Road; tel: 5404 1235; $$

This upbeat, provincial-chic diner turns out a large picture menu of fresh, well-spiced Sichuan classics, accompanied by a selection of cooling cocktails. A local expat favourite – book ahead.

### South Beauty 881

881 Central Yan'an Road; tel: 6247 6682; southbeautygroup.com/en; $$$

This impressive venue serves first-rate Sichuan food in a lavish century-old mansion and sprawling grounds. The food is genuine, tongue-searing Sichuan; the signature dish is beef cooked at the table in hot spicy oil.

### Sushi Oyama

2/F, 20 Donghu Road, near Huaihai Road; tel: 5404 7705; $$$

Fourteen-seat, reservations-only restaurant with a custom menu that changes nightly, depending on which ingredients the eponymous master chef imports fresh from Japan that day. It features the best sushi this side of Japan, and melt-in-your-mouth kobe beef, along with a selection of fine sakes.

### Tsui Wah

291 Fumin Road, near Changle Road; tel: 6170 1282; $

Reliable Cantonese favourites, plus a selection of Western dishes and a small bakery.

### Yongfoo Elite

200 Yongfu Road, near Fuxing Road; tel: 5466 2727; $$

Elegant Shanghainese flavours in an exquisitely styled former French Con-

---

Price for a two-course meal per person, with one drink:

| | |
|---|---|
| $$$ | over RMB 200 |
| $$ | RMB 100–200 |
| $ | RMB 50–100 |

cession garden villa that captures the spirit of Shanghai's 1930s heyday.

## Western Shanghai

### Dong Bei Ren

46 Panyu Road, near Yan'an Road West; tel: 5230 2230; $

Expect colourful uniforms, singing staff and over-the-top decor, along with rich and hearty meat-and-potatoes cuisine, and Harbin beer that is plentiful and cheap.

### Fu 1039

1039 Yuyuan Road, near Jiangsu Road; tel: 5237 1878; $$$

Fu 1039 serves classic Shanghainese specialities in a tucked-away heritage villa filled with antiques.

### Shen Yue Xuan

Ding Xiang Garden, 849 Huashan Road; tel: 6251 1166; $$

Quality Cantonese and Shanghainese cuisine in a pretty garden setting.

## Pudong

### Din Tai Fung

3/F, Super Brand Mall, 168 Lujiazui Road, near Oriental Pearl Tower; tel: 5047 8882; $$

This popular Taiwanese chain serves arguably Shanghai's best *xiao long bao* steamed dumplings, along with a long menu of fresh and clean-tasting regional Chinese favourites. This Pudong outlet also boasts spectacular river views.

### Face

Dongjiao State Guesthouse, 1800 Jinke Road; near Longdong Highway; tel: 5027 8261/3668; www.facebars.com; $$

A superb dining option in far-flung Pudong, this exquisite collection of restaurants in the grounds of Dongjiao State Guesthouse features four cuisines – Thai, Indian, Japanese and North African. There's also the gorgeous Face Bar, where you can sip cocktails on antique opium beds.

### Flair

58/F, The Ritz-Carlton Pudong, Shanghai IFC Tower, 8 Century Avenue; tel: 2020 1888; www.ritz carlton.com; $$$

The city's highest open-air lounge boasts a split-level terrace with spectacular views of the Oriental Pearl Tower and the Bund. Serves gourmet pan-Asian tapas from the outdoor grill, accompanied by creative cocktails and wines. Reserve ahead for one of the popular terrace perches.

### The Kitchen Salvatore Cuomo

2967 Binjiang Avenue, near Fenghe Road, Pudong; tel: 5054 1265; $$

A favourite among Italian expats living in Shanghai. Set against the waterfront under the Oriental Pearl Tower, this venue offers good views along with its pizza and perfectly cooked pasta dishes.

Midnight is the witching hour in Shanghai, when the city's night owls start to prowl the streets. The clubs and bars of choice change frequently, as newer, bigger and better-designed challengers throw open their doors. The result is a dynamic club culture that is packed with after-dark temptations, ranging from glamorous cocktail bars to DJ-fuelled dance clubs, to crowded live music bars. Shanghai is a party that doesn't stop until the sun peers over the Huangpu River, and sometimes not even then. Get dressed up and make your way to one of the following venues.

## Bars & Clubs

### Bar Rouge

7/F, 18 Zhongshan Road East No.1; tel: 6339 1199; www.bar-rouge-shanghai.com

This big Bund 18 hotspot draws upscale crowds with its cranberry-coloured lounges, hot red lighting and professional DJs – despite its famously snooty service. The best tables are on the terrace overlooking the Huangpu River; be sure to reserve or arrive early for an outside perch.

### M1NT

318 Fuzhou Road; tel: 6391 2811; www.M1NT.com.cn

Shark tanks, Bund views, beautiful people and more in this lavish club perched atop a 24-storey building behind the Bund. Entertainments include seasoned DJs, a spacious dance floor, bar, restaurant, rooftop party area and superb modern design. M1NT claims to be members-only, but go before 9.30pm and you will be ushered right in.

### M2

5/F, Plaza 66, 1266 Nanjing Road West; tel: 6288 6222; www.muse shanghai.com

Even by Shanghai standards, M2 is a monument to conspicuous consumption, where a well-heeled Shanghai and Hong Kong clientele, plus the occasional model or local celeb, dance in light-spangled splendour beneath a mirrored disco ball, lounge on acres of cushions, or hang out at the curved ivory-white bar at this 2,000-person club.

### Shanghai Studio

Building 4, 1950 Central Huaihai Road, near Wukang Road; tel: 6283 1043; www.shanghai-studio.com

A labyrinthine concrete lair in a former bomb shelter, this popular alternative hangout is known for its friendly staff, stiff drinks, welcoming vibe and over-the-top costume parties. Expect a maze of rooms, many of them featuring offbeat Asian art, a small dance floor, and a mixed local and expat crowd.

### The Shelter

5 Yongfu Road, near Fuxing Road West; tel: 6347 0400

Every city needs a nightclub like The

Shelter: concrete walls, black paint, rock-bottom drinks prices and consistently good music. This basement club draws a youthful alternative crowd, who are joined by locals looking for a good time in unpretentious surroundings.

## Velvet Lounge

913 Julu Road, near Changshu Road; tel: 5403 2976; www.cosmogroup.cn

Welcoming late-night club with good cocktails, great pizzas, atmospheric lounge nooks and a heaving dance floor. Come very early or very late if you want a seat at weekends.

## Cocktail Lounges

### Bar Constellation

251 Huangpi Road North, near Jiangyin Road; tel: 5375 2712

This 1930s-themed cocktail bar is much loved for its fine mixology. Its classic cocktails are perfectly balanced and never too sweet, and whisky and other drinks on the rocks are served "Japanese style" with a single large ice cube, so they stay cold without getting watery.

### Glamour Bar

6/F, 5 Zhongshan East (No.1) Road; tel: 6329 3751; www.m-glamour.com

A sophisticated waterfront bar below sister restaurant M on the Bund with a mirrored cocktail bar, champagne bar, wine-tasting table and superior bar bites. Jewel-coloured velvet armchairs,

Art Deco lamps and arched windows overlooking the Bund set the elegant ambience.

## The Long Bar

6/F, 2 Zhongshan East (No.1) Road; tel: 6322 9988; www.waldorfastoria shanghai.com

This legendary Shanghai watering hole dates back to the 1920s, when it was an exclusive British gentlemen's club with the longest bar in Asia. Noel Coward famously remarked that "one could see the curvature of the earth along it". Now part of Waldorf Astoria hotel, the bar has been restored to its former glory and serves well-mixed cocktails, along with fresh oysters from the Oyster Bar.

## Live Music

### Brown Sugar

Building 15, North Block Xintiandi, Lane 181 Taicang Road; tel: 5382 8998; www.brownsugarlive.com

Big, bold and beautiful, Brown Sugar is a belt-'em-out music hall with super-high ceilings, brick walls, a circular bar and roomy stage. The music here is Americana: blues, jazz, pop, showtunes and R&B, performed by a slick house band and often spiced up by visiting singers.

### LOgO

107 Sinan Road, near Taikang Road; tel: no telephone; www.logo shanghai.net

**Above from far left:** Western patrons dance and drink at the Velvet Lounge; the Glamour Bar.

A youthful favourite that is much loved for its consistent presentation of alternative music, including electronic, punk rock and metal, as well as for its gritty, smoky, laid-back interiors and reasonable cover charges. The house is packed at weekends with crowds of 20- and 30-somethings gathered for a good time.

## Theatres & Concert Halls

### Mercedes-Benz Arena

1200 Expo Avenue, Pudong; tel: 400 181 6688; www.mercedes-benz arena.com

The oyster shell-shaped performance arena on the Huangpu riverside was built for the 2010 World Expo and is the first in China to have a naming rights deal. A state-of-the-art show-place for culture, arts, sports and entertainment events, it features a multifunctional auditorium hosting everything from rock concerts to basketball games, a Cineplex, ice-skating rink and music club.

### Oriental Arts Centre

425 Dingxiang Road, Pudong; tel: 6854 1234; www.shoac.com.cn

This Paul Andreu-designed centre in Pudong has five circular halls that resemble a lotus flower in full bloom. Three theatres – a Concert Hall, Opera Hall and a smaller Performance Hall – all have superb sightlines, state-of-the-art acoustics and nature-inspired designer interiors.

### Shanghai Circus World

2266 Gonghexin Road, near Guangzhong Road; tel: 5665 3646

In the city's north, this modern arena with a revolving stage and digital water curtain, hosts *ERA: Intersection in Time*, a multimillion-dollar acrobat/circus show that runs daily.

### Shanghai Concert Hall

523 Yan'an Road East; tel: 6386 2836; www.shanghaiconcerthall.org

This venerable hall opened in 1930 as the Nanking Theatre, but in 2002 was relocated brick by brick to a new location just over 50 metres away. The classically styled beauty, now with better acoustics and a roomier stage, showcases a rich selection of performances year-round.

### Shanghai Conservatory of Music

20 Fenyang Road; tel: 6431 8542/6431 2157

Students are in the spotlight at the conservatory's He Lu Ting Concert Hall throughout the semester, and performances are open to the public free of charge. Concert schedules vary depending on the courses being offered, and on occasion, visiting musicians from Europe, North America and Asia present performances together with their students.

### Shanghai Grand Theatre

300 People's Avenue; tel: 6372

8702; www.shgtheatre.com

Opened in 1998 in People's Park, Shanghai Grand Theatre's striking design is a modern interpretation of a Chinese hall with upturned eaves that glow from within on theatre nights. It has one of the biggest and best equipped stages in Asia, and plays host to extravagant musicals such as *The Lion King* and *Cats*, while smaller performances are held in cosier side theatres.

## Film

### Grand Cinema

216 Nanjing Road West; tel: 6327 1899; www.shdgm.com

Several cinemas across town show movies in English and Chinese (check to confirm when purchasing tickets). The benefit of going to the Grand Cinema on People's Square is that you can also enjoy the fabulous Art Deco architecture of this 1933 movie theatre. There's also a rooftop lounge and mini museum.

## Jazz Venues

### Cotton Club

1416 Central Huaihai Road, corner of Fuxing Road; tel: 6437 7110

This long-running local institution presents skilled bands and tight musicianship to enthusiastic crowds. Low ceilings, lots of smoke and an aura of inky darkness add to the atmosphere, although the house band does sometimes blur the line between jazz and blues.

### House of Blues and Jazz

60 Fuzhou Road, near The Bund; tel: 6323 2779

This gem of a club in a renovated mansion on a quiet Bund backstreet attracts a firm following with its unpretentious but upscale atmosphere and excellent bands that play soul-infused blues and jazz. Its long wood-grained bar, hardwood walls and floors, and Art Deco-style fittings pay tribute to Shanghai's earlier jazz era.

### The Jazz Bar

Fairmont Peace Hotel, 20 Nanjing Road East; tel: 6321 6888; www.fairmont.com/peacehotel

A 1930s jazz institution, the dark and intimate Jazz Bar at the Peace Hotel features the original vintage jazz band (all members are aged 70+) playing timeless tunes in the early evening, followed by the more upbeat house band and guest performers, playing late into the Shanghai nights.

### JZ Club

46 Fuxing Road West; tel: 6431 0269; www.jzclub.cn

While most "jazz" venues in Shanghai play pop music and blues and even showtunes, JZ remains true to its roots, with an ongoing selection of superlative jazz musicians from China and overseas, plus a fine house band. A friendly two-storey layout, where listeners are almost on top of the stage. Book early for top bands.

**Above from far left:** Shaolin Kung Fu performers; the interior of the Grand Theatre.

| | | |
|---|---|---|
| Astor House Hotel | 浦江饭店 | Pujiang Fandian |
| Bank of China | 中国银行 | Zhongguo Yinhang |
| Broadway Mansions | 上海大厦 | Shanghai Dasha |
| Century Park | 世纪公园 | Shiji Gongyuan |
| Chenxiangge Nunnery | 沉香阁 | Chenxiang Ge |
| City God Temple | 城隍庙 | Cheng Huang Miao |
| Confucius Temple | 文庙 | Wen Miao |
| Customs House | 海关大楼 | Haiguan Dalou |
| Dongtai Road Antiques Market | 东台路古玩市场 | Dongtai Lu Guwan Shichang |
| Doulun Lu Cultural Celebrity St | 多伦路文化街 | Duolun Lu Wenhua Jie |
| Fa Zang Temple | 法藏讲寺 | Fazang Jiang Si |
| Fairmont Peace Hotel | 和平饭店 | Heping Fandian |
| Former residence of Lu Xun | 鲁迅故居 | Luxun Guju |
| Former residence of Soong | 宋庆龄故居 | Song Qingling Guju |
| Former residence of Sun Yat-sen | 孙中山故居 | Sun Zhongshan Guju |
| Former residence of Zhou en-lai | 周公馆 | Zhou Gonguan |
| Fuxing Park | 复兴公园 | Fuxing Gongyuan |
| Fuyou Road Mosque | 福佑路清真寺 | Fuyou Lu Qingzhen Si |
| Gutzlaff Signal Tower | 外滩信号台 | Waitan Xinhao Tai |
| Hengshan Moller Villa | 衡山马勒别墅 | Hengshan Male Bieshu |
| Huangpu Park | 黄浦公园 | Huangpu Gongyuan |
| Huxinting Teahouse | 湖心亭 | Huxin Ting |
| Jade Buddha Temple | 玉佛寺 | Yufo Si |
| Jing An Park | 静安公园 | Jing'an Gongyuan |
| Jing An Si | 静安寺 | Jing'an Si |
| Jinmao Tower | 金贸大厦 | Jin Mao Dasha |
| Longhua Pagoda and Temple | 龙华塔，龙华庙 | Longhua Ta, Longhua Miao |
| Lu Xun Memorial Hall | 鲁迅纪念馆 | Luxun Jinianguan |
| Lu Xun Park | 鲁迅公园 | Luxun Gongyuan |
| M Glamour | 魅力酒吧 | Meili Jiuba |
| Moore Memorial Church | 摩恩堂 | Mo'en Tang |
| Municipal Children's Palace | 上海少年宫 | Shanghai Shaonian Gong |
| Museum of Contemporary Art | 上海当代艺术馆 | Shanghai Dangdai Yishuguan |
| Oriental Arts Centre | 东方艺术中心 | Dongfang Yishu Zhongxin |
| Oriental Pearl Tower | 东方明珠 | Dongfang Mingzhu |
| Park Hotel | 国际饭店 | Guoji Fandian |
| Peninsula Shanghai | 上海半岛酒店 | Shanghai Bandao Jiudian |
| People's Park | 人民公园 | Renmin Gongyuan |

| Qinci Yangdian Temple | 钦赐仰殿道观 Qinci Yangdian Daoguan |
| Rockbund Art Museum | 上海外滩美术馆 Shanghai Waitan Meishuguan |
| Ruijin Guesthouse | 瑞金宾馆 Ruijin Binguan |
| Ohel Rachel Synagogue | 犹太教堂 Youtai Jiaotang |
| Okura Garden Hotel | 花园饭店 Huayuan Fandian |
| Shanghai Art Museum | 上海美术馆 Shanghai Meishuguan |
| Shanghai Arts & Crafts Museum | 上海工艺美术博物馆 Shanghai Gongyi Meishu Bowuguan |
| Shanghai Botanical Gardens | 上海植物园 Shanghai Zhiwuyuan |
| Shanghai Concert Hall | 上海音乐厅 Shanghai Yinyue Ting |
| Shanghai Exhibition Centre | 上海展览馆 Shanghai Zhanlanguan |
| Shanghai Grand Theatre | 上海大剧院 Shanghai Da Juyuan |
| Shanghai Jewish Refugees Museum | 犹太难民在上海纪念馆 Youtai Nanmin Zai Shanghai Jinianguan |
| Shanghai Library | 上海图书馆 Shanghai Tushuguan |
| Shanghai Municipal History Museum | 上海历史博物馆 Shanghai Lishi Bowuguan |
| Shanghai Museum | 上海博物馆 Shanghai Bowuguan |
| Shanghai Ocean Aquarium | 上海海洋水族馆 Shanghai Haiyang Shuizuguan |
| Shanghai Postal Museum | 上海邮政博物馆 Shanghai Youzheng Bowuguan |
| Shanghai Pudong Development Bank | 上海浦发银行 Shanghai Pufa Yinhang |
| Shanghai Science & Technology Museum | 上海科技馆 Shanghai Keji Guan |
| Shanghai Urban Planning Centre | 上海城市规划馆 Shanghai Chengshi Guihua Guan |
| Shanghai World Financial Centre | 上海国际金融中心 Shanghai Guoji Jinrong Zhongxin |
| Site of the First National Congress of the Communist Party of Shanghai | 中共一大会址 Zhonggong Yida Huizhi |
| Waibaidu Bridge | 外白渡桥 Waibaidu Qiao |
| Waitanyuan | 外滩源 WaitanYuan |
| Waldorf Astoria Hotel | 外滩华尔道夫饭店 Waitan Hua'erdaofu Fandian |
| Wanshang Bird and Flower Market | 万商花鸟市场 Wanshang Huaniao Shichang |
| Xiahai Temple | 下海庙 Xiahai Miao |
| Xintiandi | 新天地 Xin Tian Di |
| Xujiahui Cathedral | 徐家汇教堂 Xujiahui Jiaotang |
| Yifu Theatre | 逸夫舞台 Yifu Wutai |
| Yu Garden | 豫园 Yuyuan |

**Above:** street sign for Nanjing Road West.

# CREDITS

**Insight Step by Step Shanghai**
**Written by**: Tina Kanagaratnam and
Amy Fabris-Shi
**Series Editor**: Carine Tracanelli
**Editor**: Tom Le Bas
**Cartography Editors**: Zoë Goodwin
and James Macdonald
**Map Production**: Stephen Ramsay and Apa
Cartography Department
**Production**: Linton Donaldson
**Picture research and design**: Corrie Wingate
**Photography**: David Shen Kai/Apa Publications 2TC,
2BC, 4TL, 4CL, 6TL, 7TR, 7CR, 7BL, 7BR, 8/9, 8C,
8CR, 12/13T, 13TL, 15TL, 16T, 19TR, 22/23T, 25TL,
26/27, 26TC, 26BL, 28/29T, 30TL,30/31T, 31TR, 32TL,
33TR, 36TL, 37TR, 38/39T, 38BL, 40TL, 41TR, 42TL,
44TL, 44/45T, 45TR, 47TR, 48TL, 48/49T, 50TL,
51TR, 53TR, 54TL, 54/55T, 55TR, 56TL, 57TR, 58TL,
58/59T, 59TR, 60TL, 60/61T, 61TR, 61CL, 62TL,
65TR, 66CL, 66BL, 67TR, 69TR, 70TL, 71TR, 77TR,
82TL, 84TL, 84/85T, 85TR, 84CL, 84BL, 86TL, 87TR,
88BL, 89TR, 90TL, 90/91T, 91BR, 92/93, 92TL, 92TC,
96TL, 96/97T, 97TR, 101TR, 103TR, 109TR, 110TL,
110/111T, 111TR, 114TL, 120TL, 121TR; Ryan Pyle/
Apa Publications 2/3, 2TL, 2TR, 2BL, 2BR, 4LC, 4LB,
6CR, 6CL, 6BR, 6BL, 7CL, 8TL, 8BL, 8CB, 8BR,
10TL, 11TR, 12TL, 15BL, 17T, 18TL, 18/19T, 19TR,
19BR, 23BR, 26TL, 26TR, 26BC, 26BR, 28TR, 34/35T,
35TR, 38TL, 39TR, 40BR, 42/43T, 43TR, 46TL, 49TR,
50/51T, 52TL, 56/57T, 63TR, 64TL, 64BL, 66TL, 68TL,
70BL, 72TL, 72/73T, 73TR, 74TL, 74/75T, 75TR, 76TL,
76/77T, 92TR, 92BL, 92BC, 92BR, 94TL, 95TR, 98TL,
98/99T, 99TR, 100TL, 102TL, 104TL, 104TR, 110TL,
114/115T, 115TR, 118TL, 119TR, 122/123T; Alex
Havret/Apa Publications 14TL, 62B, 91T; Ddnyddny/
Dreamstime 80B; Fzy826/Dreamstime 78T, 80T; Leon-
ardo 23TR, 106T, 107T, 108TL, 108/109T, 111T; Mark
Buxton/iStockphoto 34TL; Mary Evans Picture Library
24T, 24B; Mauriehill/Dreamstime 83T; Photoshot 21;
Richard and Abe Nowitz/Apa Pubications 14/15T; Ritz-
Carlton 116/117(all); Starwood 109TL; Thomas von
Aesch/iStockphoto 28TL; Vanbeets/Dreamstime 88T;
YellowRiver2011/iStockphoto 81B; Zhangjinsong/
Dreamstime 79T, 81T.; Zhiwei Zhou/Dreamstime 20
**Front cover**: main image: AWL Images; bottom
left: iStockphoto; bottom right: iStockphoto.
**Printed by**: CTPS-China

## CONTACTING THE EDITORS

We would appreciate it if readers would alert us to
errors or outdated information by writing to us
at insight@apaguide.co.uk or APA Publications,
PO Box 7910, London SE1 1WE, UK.

## DISTRIBUTION

*Worldwide*
**APA Publications GmbH & Co. Verlag KG
(Singapore branch)**
7030 Ang Mo Kio Ave 5
08-65 Northstar @ AMK, Singapore 569880
Email: apasin@singnet.com.sg

*UK and Ireland*
**Dorling Kindersley Ltd**
(a Penguin Company)
80 Strand, London, WC2R 0RL, UK
Email: customerservice@uk.dk.com
*United States*

www.insightguides.com

**Ingram Publisher Services**
One Ingram Blvd, PO Box 3006
La Vergne, TN 37086-1986
Email: customer.service@
ingrampublisherservices.com

*Australia*
**Universal Publishers**
PO Box 307

St. Leonards NSW 1590
Email: sales@universalpublishers.com.au

*New Zealand*
**Brown Knows Publications**
11 Artesia Close, Shamrock Park
Auckland, New Zealand 2016
Email: sales@brownknows.co.nz

# INDEX